WAR DEPARTMENT. ORDNANCE OFFICE,
WASHINGTON. MARCH 17. 1942.

ORDNANCE FIELD SERVICE TECHNICAL
BULLETIN NO. 23-7-1

CARBINE, CAL. .30, M1

•

TABLE OF CONTENTS

CARBINE, CAL. .30, M1
SECTION I
INTRODUCTION

1.   SCOPE. — *a.* This technical bulletin is published for the information and guidance of those concerned pending the publication of FM 23-7 and TM 9-1276.

b. In addition to a description of the Carbine, Cal. .30, M1, this technical bulletin contains information required for the identification, use and care of the materiel and its component accessories, including available information on ammunition.

c. Disassembly, assembly, and such repairs as may be handled by using arms personnel will be undertaken only under the supervision of an officer or the chief mechanic.

d. In all cases where the nature of the repair, modification or adjustment is beyond the scope or facilities of the unit, the responsible ordnance service should be informed in order that trained personnel with suitable tools and equipment may be provided, or proper instructions issued.

2.   DESCRIPTION. — *a.* The Carbine, Cal. .30, M1 *(Figures 1, 2 and 3)* is a gas-operated, self-loading, air-cooled, shoulder weapon, delivering semi-automatic fire controlled ·by the operator. It is fed by a box magazine containing 15 cartridges staggered in the magazine. The weapon has an over-all length of approximately 36 inches and weighs approximately 5.80 pounds with sling and loaded magazine attached.

b. The carbine is in many ways similar in operation, functioning, and general design to the U. S. Rifle, Cal. .30, M1, and, in general, is composed of four main groups of assemblies and parts: the barrel and receiver, the trigger mechanism, the operating mechanism, and the stock, hand guard and sling.

(1) *Barrel group.* — (a) The barrel is 18 inches long, cylindrical and without taper for two-thirds of its length. It is threaded into the forward end of the receiver, and in the rear face is a cut to furnish clearance for the extractor. To the muzzle end is attached the front sight group composed of a ring body with an integral blade, positioned midway between two side wings keyed and pinned to the barrel.

(b) A gas cylinder is positioned on the underside of the barrel near the chamber and contains the piston, locked in by the piston nut, which limits its rearward movement. A gas port is drilled at an angle through the gas cylinder and barrel, entering the bore about 4½ inches from the rear face of the barrel. This rearward positioning of the gas cylinder and port makes it possible to take the gas from the bore close to the chamber, before cooling can take place, thus minimizing carbonization.

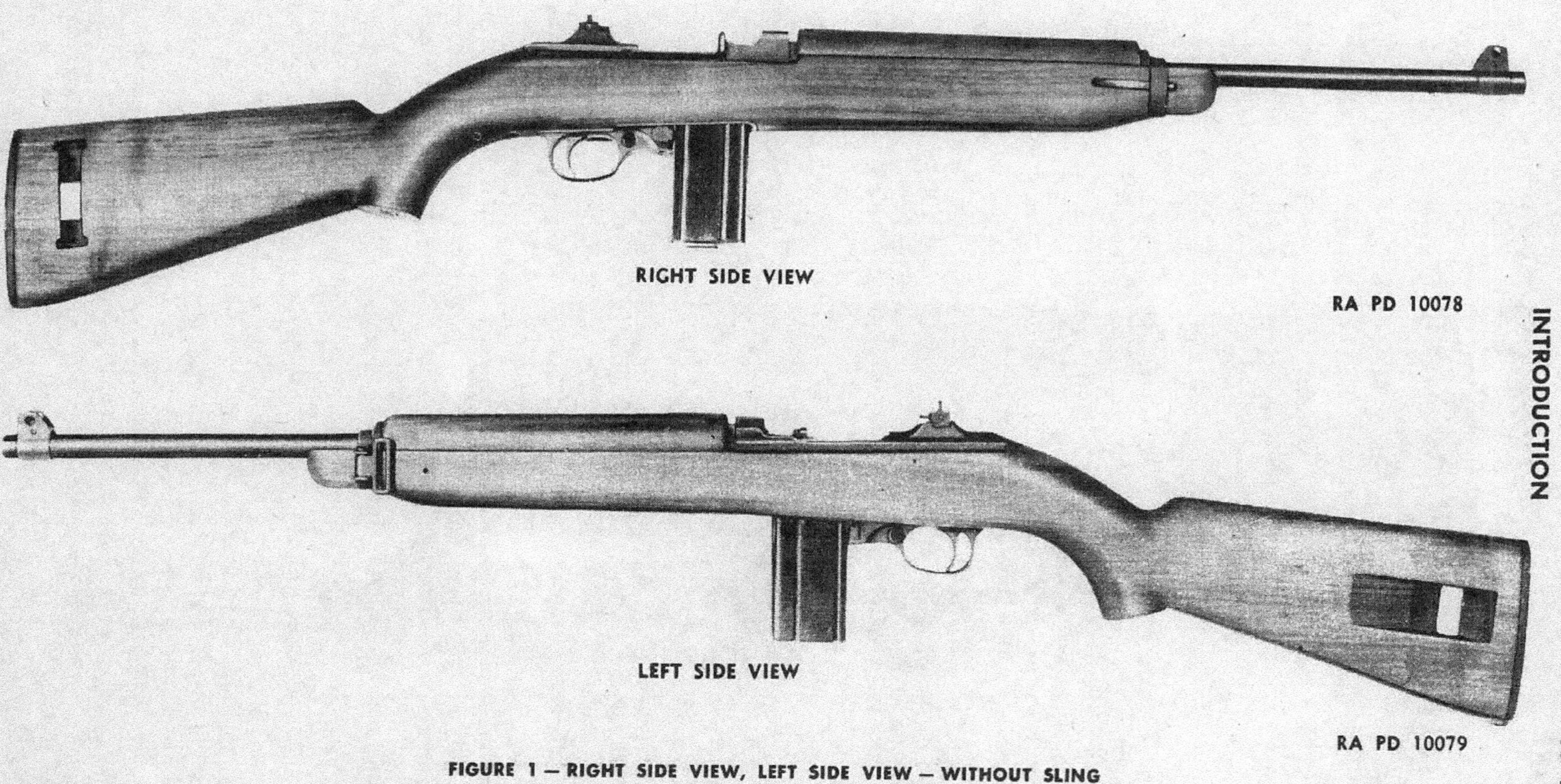

FIGURE 1 — RIGHT SIDE VIEW, LEFT SIDE VIEW — WITHOUT SLING

CARBINE, CAL. .30, M1

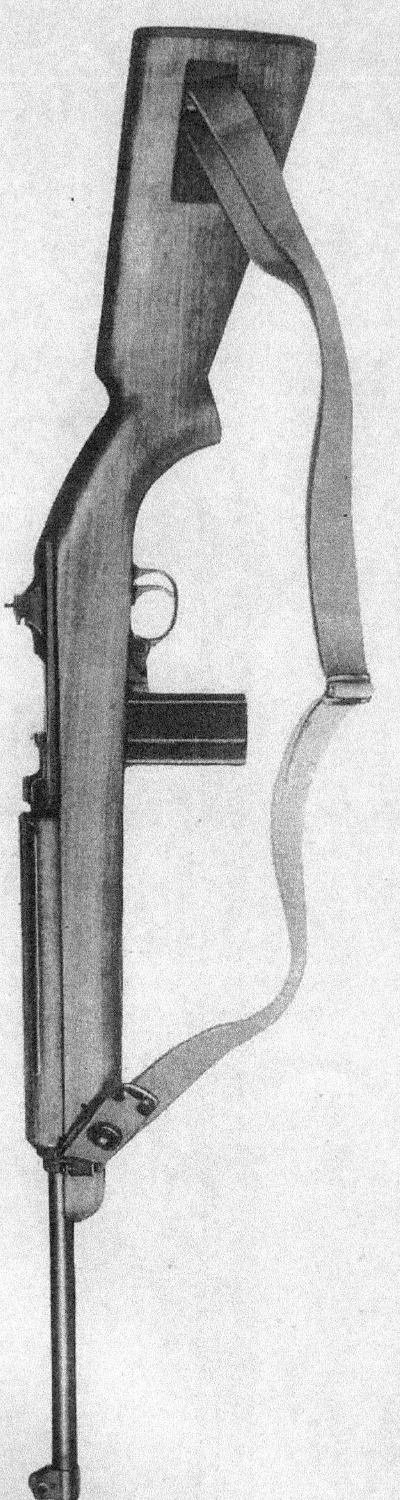

RA PD 10727

FIGURE 2 — LEFT SIDE VIEW — WITH SLING

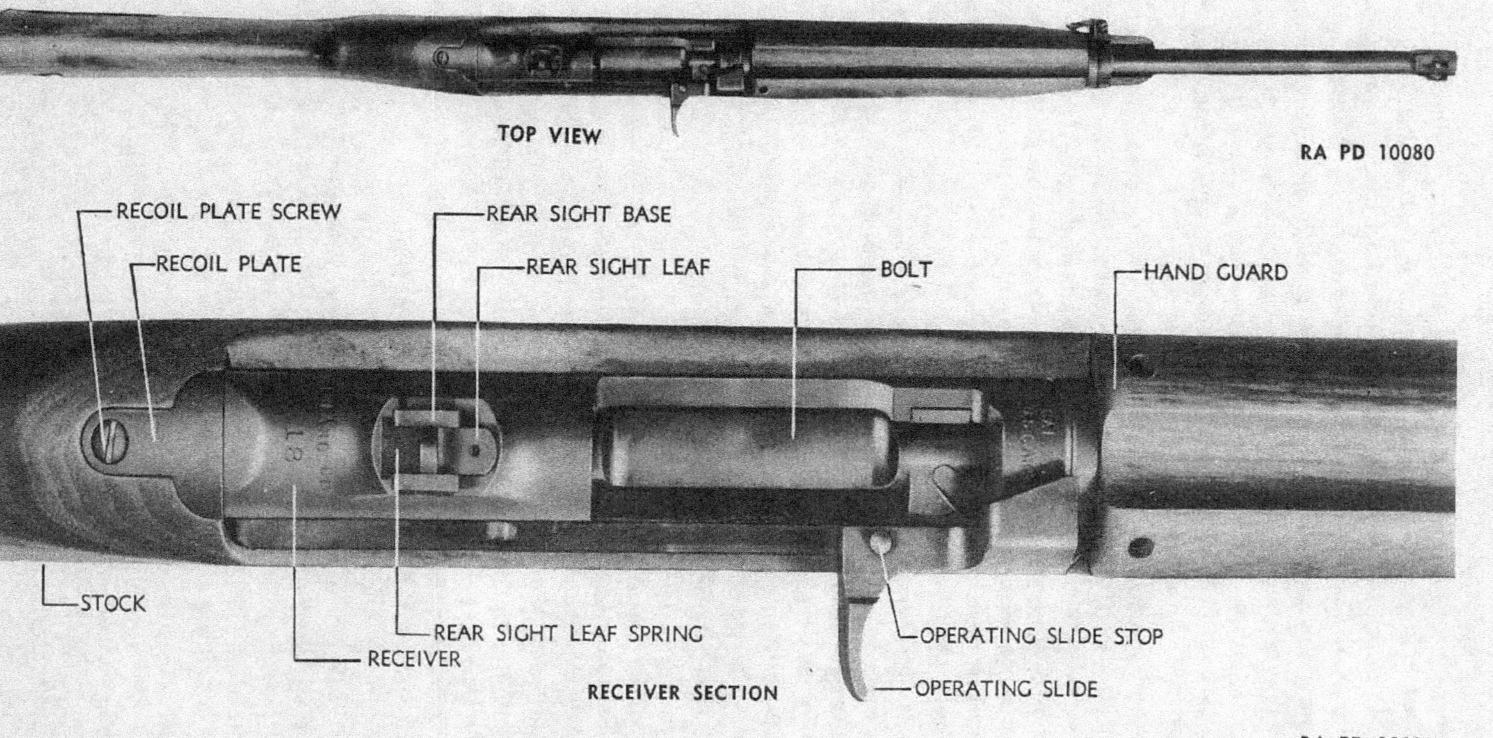

FIGURE 3 — TOP VIEW — RECEIVER SECTION

CARBINE, CAL. .30, M1

At this time there are two types of barrel and gas cylinder. In the first type the barrel and gas cylinder are integral; in the second type the gas cylinder slides onto the barrel and is retained in position by a pin.

(c) On the lower sides of the barrel, to the rear of the gas cylinder, parallel guide grooves are cut, which mate with guide lugs on the body of the operating slide to form a guideway for the operating slide and hold it in position. In the left hand barrel groove is a relief cut, by means of which the slide body is positioned and removed. (Refer to subparagraph (3) *(d)* below).

(2) *Receiver group.* — *(a)* The receiver is of one piece, open at top and bottom, and contains the operating mechanism, and to it the trigger housing (mechanism) is attached. In the inner sides of the receiver parallel bolt guide grooves are cut, in which the bolt reciprocates, and bolt lug locking apertures which are cut with a shoulder which holds the bolt locked in the closed position when cam-rotated by the operating slide at the end of the forward movement.

(b) On the right outer side of the receiver is the operating slide retaining groove in which the rear end (handle) lug of the operating slide reciprocates when the slide is actuated by the piston and operating slide spring respectively. In the top of this groove is a relief cut, by means of which the rear end (handle) of the operating slide is disengaged from the bolt. Slightly to the rear and below this relief cut is an aperture for seating the operating slide stop.

(c) On the rear face of the receiver is a lug which engages in an undercut in the recoil plate (mounted in the stock) to lock the rear end of the barrel and receiver group to the stock. Below this lug, on the underside of the receiver, are two L-shaped lugs into which a T-lug on the rear end of the trigger housing slides and is retained. On the forward end of the receiver is a straight lug with a pin hole which alines with pin holes in a mating U-lug on the forward end of the trigger housing. Through these alined pin holes the trigger housing retaining pin passes to hold the trigger housing in position.

(d) In the bridge of the receiver an aperture is cut with which the tang of the firing pin must mate in order to move forward in the bolt. This mating cannot be accomplished until the bolt is rotated to the locked position.

(e) On the top rear of the receiver is the rear sight group composed of a base (dovetailed into the receiver), leaf, spring, and pin. The leaf is an L-shaped piece, consisting of two leaves set at right angles to each other, each pierced with an aperture at a different height. The leaf can be rotated 90° on the leaf pin, thus positioning one or the other of the integral leaves, thereby giving sight elevations for two range limits. This construction necessitates one leaf remaining upright at all times. When the *low* leaf is perpendicular, the carbine is sighted up to 200 yards,

INTRODUCTION

and when the *high* leaf is perpendicular, up to 300 yards. (For shot grouping at 100 and 300 yards, refer to paragraph 50 c).

(f) In the under side of the receiver is an aperture into which the magazine fits, and is retained by the magazine catch positioned in the trigger housing.

(3) *Operating mechanism group.* — *(a)* The operating mechanism is composed of the bolt, the operating slide, operating slide spring, and spring guide. The bolt operates within the receiver, and the operating slide in its grooves on the right outside face of the receiver and lower rear faces of barrel.

(b) The bolt contains the firing pin, extractor and ejector groups and is connected to the operating slide by a lug on its right side, which mates with a camming aperture in the left face of the operating slide (handle). In line with this lug, and similarly placed on each side of the bolt, are locking lugs which engage in the receiver locking apertures already described.

(c) The extractor is of the claw type, seated in an aperture in the top of the bolt and actuated by a plunger and spring. The ejector is seated in a well in the lower part of the bolt, locked in by the extractor and actuated by a spring. The firing pin is seated in a well in the center of the bolt, is locked in by the extractor, and has a tang on the rear end which blocks it from functioning until the bolt is locked, as already explained.

(d) The operating slide is composed of an integral body and (retracting) handle. The body reciprocates in its guideways on the under side of the barrel, and the handle in its guideway in the right outside face of the receiver. The function of the slide is to move the bolt backward and forward unlocking it from, and locking it to, the receiver at the proper time. The bolt in turn cocks the hammer on its rearward movement and feeds the cartridge into the chamber on its forward movement. The force to accomplish these actions is supplied by the backward thrust of the piston on the recoil stroke and the forward thrust of the loaded operating slide spring on the counterrecoil stroke. The operating slide is provided with a retracting handle for retracting the bolt. On the shank of the handle is a lug which contains the aforementioned bolt lug camming aperture. To the rear of this lug is the guide lug. The operating slide spring seats in a well in the forward face of the receiver, and acts on the operating spring guide, the forward end of which seats in an indentation in the rear face of the operating slide (body). In the rear end of the operating slide (handle) is a stop, operated by a spring. The stop hangs the bolt when depressed and held into its retaining aperture in the operating slide (handle) guideway in the receiver.

(4) *Trigger mechanism group.* — *(a)* The trigger (housing) mechanism group is composed of the trigger housing, trigger, hammer and sear, together

with their component springs and pins, and the hammer spring plunger. The trigger housing is attached to the receiver at the rear, by means of a lug on the rear end of the trigger housing which engages with L-shaped mating lugs on the lower rear face of the receiver. The front end of the housing is held in position by a retaining pin passing through mating lugs on the forward end of the receiver and trigger housing and held in position by a spring. (Refer to subparagraph *b* (2) *(c)*, above).

(*b*) The trigger and sear rotate about the trigger pin and the hammer about the hammer pin. The hammer spring plunger seats in a notch in the rear face of the hammer shank and extends through an aperture in the rear of the trigger guard body, while the hammer spring bears upon the trigger housing and a collar on the plunger. The trigger spring is a U-shaped spring which fits in a slot in the rear end of the trigger, and an aperture in the rear end of the trigger housing. The rear end of the sear spring is seated in a well in the trigger body, the forward end in an aperture in the rear face of the sear.

(*c*) A safety is housed in the forward end of the trigger housing just forward of the bow. The safety is in the form of a cylindrical pin with a cut so fashioned that it clears or blocks the forward end of the trigger when the safety is pushed from side to side in its aperture. The safety is held in position by the safety plunger and spring. On the right side of the trigger housing, just ahead of the safety, is the magazine catch. This catch functions in an aperture in the forward face of the trigger housing, and is held in engagement with two small lugs on the magazine by the magazine catch spring and plunger. The catch, when pressed, moves laterally to disengage it from the magazine lugs so that the magazine may be removed from the receiver.

(5) *Stock, hand guard and sling group.* —(*a*) The stock group is composed of the stock in which the receiver and barrel are bedded, and the hand guard, positioned on top of the barrel forward of the receiver. In the rear of the aperture in which the receiver is bedded, the recoil plate is positioned. This plate is secured to the stock by the recoil plate screw passing through the tang of the recoil plate and thence through the grip of the stock, and threaded into an escutcheon let into the underside of the stock grip. The recoil plate serves to lock the rear end of the receiver to the stock as heretofore described, and to protect the wood of the stock from the hammering of the recoil mechanism. A recessed butt plate is screwed to the butt end of the stock by a wood screw.

(*b*) To the rear end of the hand guard a metal liner is riveted, which protrudes slightly beyond the wood of the hand guard. This liner, when mated with an undercut in the top forward face of the receiver, secures the rear end of the hand guard to the receiver. The forward end is secured to the barrel by the front band which slides over the barrel and forward end of the stock and hand guard, thus securing all

INTRODUCTION

three together. The band is locked in position by a locking spring and screw.

(c) A web sling is attached to a sling swivel mounted on the left side of the front band. In the rear end of the sling a loop is formed by means of a metal button passing through two button holes in the sling (recent style). This loop passes from the left side around the oiler, which seats in the right side of an aperture cut through the stock near the butt. The dimensions of the aperture through which the oiler is inserted prevents it falling out after the sling has been passed around it. Thus the oiler is held in the aperture by the sling, and acts as an anchor pin for the rear end of the sling. To the forward end of the sling a locking buckle is attached, by which adjustment of the sling is attained, after it has passed through the sling swivel.

NOTE: The oiler is cylindrical in shape and has a screw top to which a dropper rod is attached. It is used for lubricating the carbine as well as to hold the sling in position.

c. The magazine is composed of a tube, base, follower, and spring. When loaded, the cartridges lie staggered in the tube and are pushed into line with the bolt, at the mouth of the tube, by the action of the follower and the follower spring. The mouth of the tube is narrower than the body of the tube and has its lips crimped inward. Thus one cartridge at a time is positioned and held in line with the bolt, ready to be pushed forward and loaded into the chamber as the bolt moves forward on the counterrecoil stroke.

3. DATA. —

Weight of carbine with magazine (unloaded)	pounds	5.19
Weight of carbine with magazine (loaded) and sling	pounds	5.80
Weight of magazine (unloaded)	pounds	.17
Weight of magazine (loaded) with 15 cartridges	pounds	.59
Weight of 100 cartridges	pounds	2.79
Weight of 1 cartridge	grains	195
Magazine capacity	rounds	15
Over-all length of carbine	inches	36
Length of barrel	inches	18
Rifling, R.H., one turn in	inches	20
Grooves in barrel	number	4
Sight radius	inches	21.46
Trigger pull	pounds	4-6
Ballistics of cartridge	(Refer to Section VII — Ammunition)	

NOTE: 7000 grains equal 1 pound avoirdupois measure.

CARBINE, CAL. .30, M1

SECTION II

OPERATION AND FUNCTIONING

4. GENERAL. — Operation and functioning will, for convenience, be divided into two main groups of actions: the manual operations necessary to load, fire and unload the weapon, and the mechanical functioning of the mechanisms when acted upon by the force generated by the expanding powder gas when the cartridge is fired.

5. TO LOAD THE MAGAZINE. — Insert 15 cartridges into the magazine one at a time. To insert cartridge, hold magazine in the left hand with the curved, open end up and to the right. Grasp a cartridge in the right hand between thumb and forefinger with base to the left. Insert base of cartridge in right end of opening in top of magazine and press down with thumb against follower, forcing cartridge below lips of magazine. Then push cartridge to left, beneath lips, until base of cartridge contacts rear of magazine tube. Grasp another cartridge in the same manner and press down upon the first cartridge and slide the second cartridge to the left over the first one. Continue thus until all the 15 cartridges are loaded into the clip. The cartridges will be staggered in the magazine when it is fully loaded, with the top cartridge centered between the lips of the magazine. If the follower does not depress smoothly, push down and release a few times. If this does not improve the action, look for dents, rust or foreign matter in magazine tube, or for bent follower.

6. TO LOAD THE CARBINE. — *a.* Insert a loaded magazine into opening in receiver with the retaining lugs (flat face) to the rear and push it up until the magazine catch snaps into position, below the retaining lugs on the rear face of the magazine tube. If magazine does not snap in easily, depress the catch. Ordinarily this action should be performed with the bolt locked and the hammer let down. This makes it possible to carry the carbine safely with loaded magazine attached, as it cannot be fired until the bolt is retracted and allowed to close and lock.

b. With loaded magazine latched in position, retract the bolt, with little finger *(Figure 4)*, all the way to rear by pulling back the operating slide handle, and then allow it to snap forward. Unless the bolt is fully

OPERATION AND FUNCTIONING

retracted, the sear may not be seated properly in the sear notch in the hammer. The carbine is now fully loaded with a cartridge in the chamber and the hammer cocked. To fire the carbine it is now only necessary to pull the trigger and thus release the hammer. When thus loaded, unless the carbine is to be fired immediately, the firing mechanism should be placed at *safe* by pushing the safety all the way to the right. When thus placed at safe, the safety must be pushed all the way to the left before the trigger can be pulled to fire the weapon. (For sight setting, refer to paragraph 2 *b* (2) *(e)*).

7. TO UNLOAD THE CARBINE.— a. Press the magazine catch to the left and withdraw the magazine from the receiver (*Figure 5*). Magazine will usually fall out.

b. Retract the bolt fully by pulling back the operating slide handle. As the bolt moves to the rear it will extract the cartridge seated in the chamber and eject it. The live cartridge case can be prevented from being thrown clear of the receiver by the ejector, and so possibly damaged, by placing the thumb over the receiver, thus blocking the throw of the cartridge. If cartridge is ejected freely, it should be wiped clean of foreign matter before reloading it into the magazine. Examine chamber to see that it is empty before allowing bolt to go forward and close. This is always a safe practice when retracting the bolt, to obviate the possibility of a cartridge being left in the chamber. Ordinarily the bolt should be allowed to close slowly on an empty chamber and not to snap shut.

c. When it is determined beyond doubt that the chamber is empty, and with the magazine removed from the receiver, remove the tension from the hammer spring by pulling the trigger and letting the hammer down. If this is done while the bolt is still partly retracted, the hammer blow on the firing pin will be lessened and the hammer will be let down easily as the bolt closes. The hammer should *never* be so released when there is a loaded cartridge in the chamber.

d. To unload the chamber without withdrawing the magazine, retract the bolt, block the extracted cartridge as explained and lift from the receiver. Before allowing the bolt to go forward, depress the top cartridge in the magazine with the thumb so that the bolt will ride over it in closing. Allow the bolt to close slowly, watching to see that it slides over the top cartridge and closes on an empty chamber. As a rule, however, the magazine should be removed, unless empty, before chamber is unloaded.

8. TO OPERATE THE CARBINE AS A SINGLE LOADER. — With *empty* magazine in place, retract bolt fully and place a cartridge in the chamber. Allow bolt to close smartly so that extractor will engage base of cartridge and bolt be rotated to full lock. Where noise is a factor, the bolt may be eased to the closed position and the operating slide

CARBINE, CAL. .30, M1

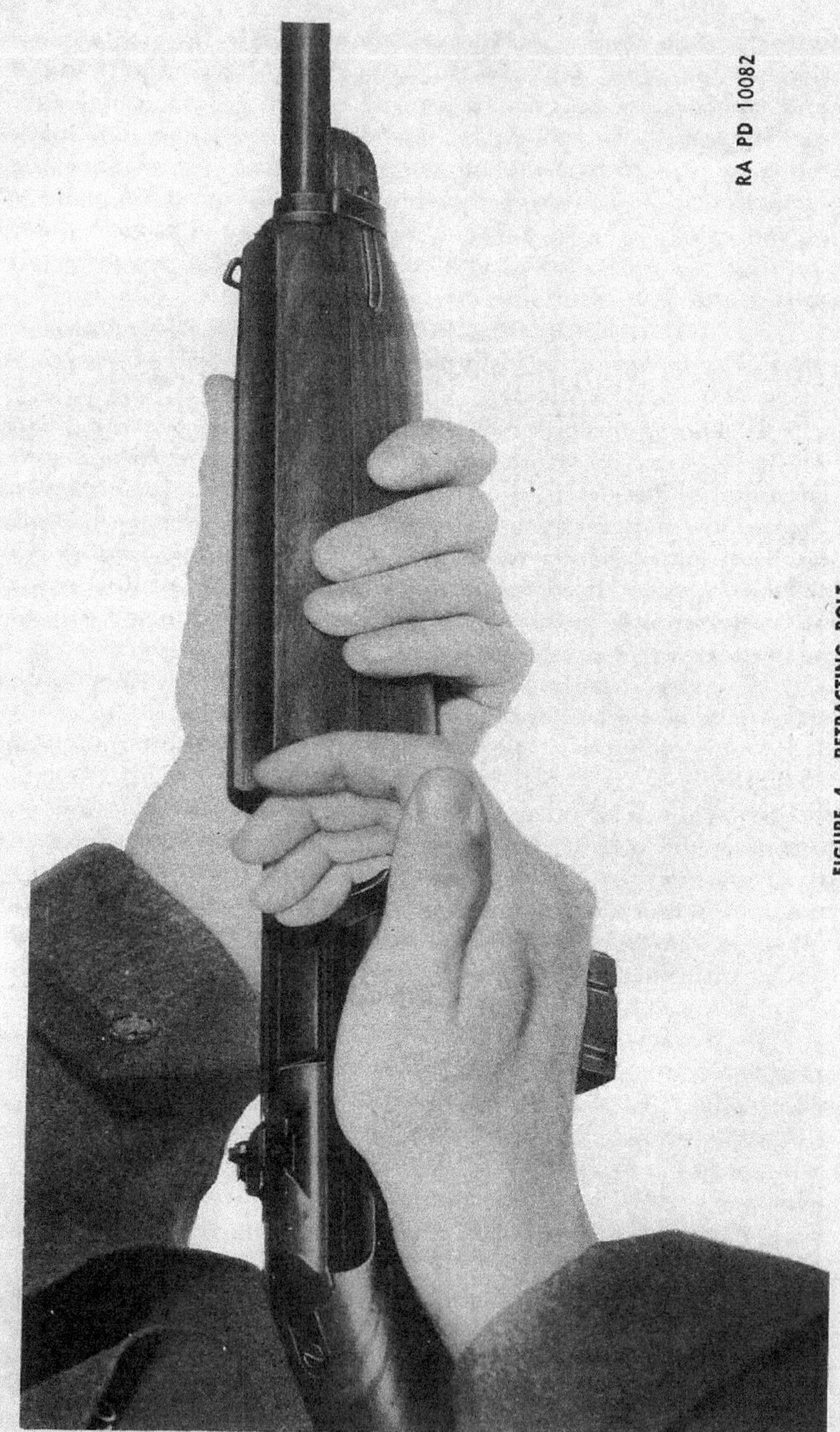

RA PD 10082

FIGURE 4 — RETRACTING BOLT

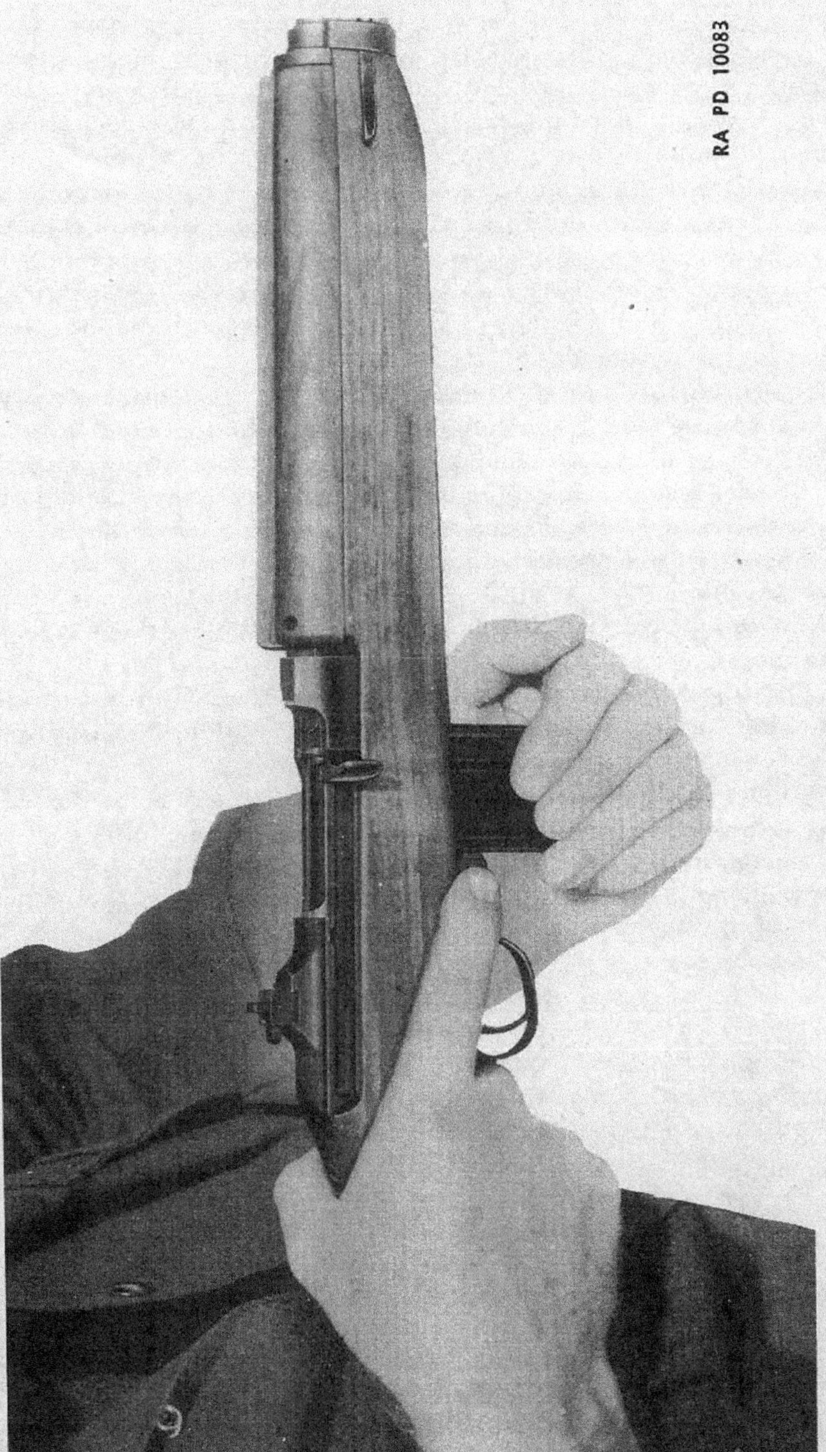

FIGURE 5 — REMOVING MAGAZINE

handle pressed forward at the end of the movement to insure complete locking of the bolt. Unless carbine is to be fired immediately, the firing mechanism should be placed at *safe*, by pressing safety fully to right. To unload, retract bolt fully to the rear, to eject cartridge, and examine chamber to make sure it is empty, before allowing to close.

CAUTION: During the operation of loading and unloading and placing firing mechanism on *safe*, the muzzle of the carbine should be pointed down, and care exercised to see that it is not pointing at the foot or anything that could be damaged in case the carbine fires accidentally. Care should always be observed when handling weapons whether loaded or unloaded.

9. INDIVIDUAL SAFETY PRECAUTIONS. — a. Consider every carbine to be loaded until you have examined it and proved it to be unloaded. Never trust your memory as to its condition in this respect.

b. Never point the carbine at anyone you do not intend to shoot, nor in a direction where an accidental discharge may do harm.

c. Always fully unload the carbine if it is to be left where someone else may handle it.

d. Always point the carbine up when snapping the trigger after examination.

e. .If it is desired to carry the carbine cocked, with a cartridge in the chamber, the trigger should be blocked by pushing the safety to the right.

f. Under no circumstances should the hammer be let down on a partially closed bolt, with a cartridge in the chamber.

g. Never fire a carbine with any grease, cleaning patch, dust, dirt, mud, snow, or other obstruction in the bore. To do so may burst the barrel or blow the bolt.

h. Never grease or oil the ammunition. This may affect the ammunition, and creates a hazardous pressure on the carbine bolt. (Refer to paragraph 51).

i. Chamber and bore should be wiped dry of oil or grease before firing for the reason given in g and h above.

j. See that ammunition is clean and dry. Examine all live and dummy ammunition. Turn in all cartridges with loose bullets or which appear to be otherwise defective.

k. Do not allow ammunition to be exposed to the direct rays of the sun for any length of time. This creates hazardous chamber pressure.

10. REARWARD MOVEMENT OF THE OPERATING MECHANISM. — In the following description of the mechanical functioning of the carbine, it is assumed that the carbine has just been fired and that there is a full or partially full magazine in the carbine.

a. As the bullet passes down the bore, propelled by the force of the expanding powder gas, it passes the gas port in the bore. As the

OPERATION AND FUNCTIONING

bullet clears the port some of the highly compressed gas, propelling it, passes through the port into the gas cylinder and acts upon the head of the piston. The piston is driven rearward a short distance (about ¼ inch) where it is stopped by contact with the piston nut which locks it in the gas cylinder. The rearward motion of the piston is transferred to the operating slide, the forward face of which has been bearing upon the rear face of the piston. The operating slide is thus driven rearward, carrying with it the bolt with which it is engaged.

    b. Before starting its rearward movement, the bolt is rotated slightly through the camming action of the cam aperture in the operating slide (handle) lug with which it is engaged. This cammed rotation disengages the locking lugs of the bolt from the corresponding apertures in the receiver and allows the bolt to be moved to the rear by the operating slide. During this rearward movement the operating slide compresses the operating slide spring, which seats in its well in the forward face of the receiver and through its guide bears on the rear face of the operating slide body. The compression of this spring furnishes the power for the forward movement of slide and bolt.

    c. As the bolt moves rearward it withdraws the empty cartridge case from the chamber, gripped in the extractor. As the forward end of the empty case clears the receiver, the ejector (in face of the bolt) which has been held under compression against the base of the cartridge case, throws the case off the bolt and out of the receiver.

    d. While moving to the rear, the rear face of the bolt bears against the forward face of the hammer and thus drives the hammer back and down, rotating it about the hammer pin, until the sear notch of the hammer is in position to be engaged by the nose of the sear. At this point the nose of the sear engages in the sear notch in the hammer and is held in engagement (due to the elongation of the pivot hole) by the pressure of the sear spring, as the bolt rides back over the hammer, for a short distance, to the end of its rearward movement.

    11. FORWARD MOVEMENT OF THE OPERATING MECHANISM. — When the bolt has reached the limit of its rearward (recoil) movement, it starts forward, propelled by the operating slide. The energy for the forward (counterrecoil) movement of the slide and bolt is furnished by the operating slide spring which was compressed (loaded) during the rearward movement of the operating slide. The bolt, moving forward, strikes the base of a cartridge which was centrally positioned in the mouth of the magazine by the magazine follower and spring, after the bolt passed over it during the rearward movement. As the bolt continues forward it pushes the cartridge out of the magazine and into the chamber of the barrel. As the bolt slams shut on the seated cartridge, the extractor is cammed open and its claw then slips into the cannelure in the base of the cartridge. At the same time the ejector, in the face of the bolt, is compressed against its spring by the base of the cartridge. As the bolt moves farther forward, it is rotated by the cam in the operating slide (handle) lug so that, upon closing, its locking lugs are in position in front of the locking shoulders of the receiver. The tang of the firing pin is now in position to mate with the slot in the receiver and be driven forward to fire the cartridge when the hammer is released.

12. ACTION OF THE TRIGGER MECHANISM. — *a.* The recoil of the bolt is completed so rapidly that the operator has not usually had time to release the trigger. Thus the trigger is still in the rearward position when the hammer is driven back and down (cocked) by the bolt on its rearward (recoil) movement. In this rearward position, the rear end of the trigger is raised and the trigger spring compressed. The sear spring, however, has forced the sear forward, as the (trigger) pin hole in the sear is in the form of an elongated slot. The forward movement of the sear has caused the rear end of the sear to drop below the level of the lip on the rear (top) of the trigger. As the hammer is forced back and down, rotating on its pin by the rearward movement of the bolt, the lower (curved) surface of the hammer rides over the top of the sear until the sear notch in the hammer is in position to be engaged by the sear. At this point the sear spring forces the nose of the sear into engagement with the sear notch in the hammer. The elongated (trigger) pin hole in the sear allows the sear to remain in engagement with the hammer even when the hammer is forced back beyond the cocking point by the bolt riding over it, in completing the rearward movement.

b. When the trigger is released, the trigger spring forces its rear end downward, and the hammer spring, acting through the hammer, forces the sear to the rear. This rearward movement of the sear is made possible by the elongated (trigger) pin hole in the sear. The release of the trigger has allowed the lip on its rear (top) end to drop low enough for the sear to ride over, and rest upon it.

c. If the trigger is now retracted (squeezed), the rear end will rise, carrying with it the rear end of the sear which is now resting upon it. The sear, pivoting about the trigger pin, will have its forward end forced down and thus out of engagement with the sear notch in the hammer. The hammer is thus free to rotate about the hammer pin. It is forced forward by the hammer spring plunger, propelled by the force of the compressed hammer spring, and strikes the tang of the firing pin. The firing pin is thus driven forward to strike the primer which fires the cartridge and starts a new functioning cycle.

d. In moving forward, the tang of the firing pin must clear a slot in the bridge of the receiver, which can only be done when the bolt is fully rotated to the locked position. If the hammer should strike the firing pin when the bolt is in any other position, the effect would be to deaden the hammer blow, and to rotate the bolt towards its locked position.

e. The carbine is provided with a safety, located in the bow of the trigger housing just forward of the trigger. When it is positioned to the left, a slot in the safety permits the forward end of the trigger to be depressed, thus allowing the rear end to rise. If the safety is positioned to the right, the solid part of the safety blocks the forward end of the trigger, and prevents it from being depressed. Thus the rear end cannot rise and the hammer cannot be released.

f. The magazine is composed of a tube, base, follower and spring. The spring is positioned in the tube between the base and the follower so that when the follower is forced towards the bottom of the tube the spring is compressed. The compression of the spring furnishes the force for feeding the cartridges into position at the mouth of the tube. The cartridges are loaded into the magazine tube one at a time, as described in "To load the magazine," paragraph 5. The magazine is held in position in the bottom of the receiver by the magazine catch as already described.

CARBINE, CAL. .30, M1

SECTION III

DISASSEMBLY AND ASSEMBLY

13. GENERAL. — *a.* Disassembly and assembly is treated herein under two general heads: removal and replacement of groups to the extent required for cleaning, adjustment and minor repairs, and detailed disassembly and assembly of the component parts of each group.

b. When disassembling, attention should be paid to position and manner of removal of groups and parts as an aid to assembly. A group is a number of parts which either function together or are intimately related to each other and should, therefore, be considered together.

c. Disassembled groups and parts should be placed upon a clean, flat surface and care observed to guard against loss of pins, springs and other small parts. All parts should be thoroughly cleaned and oiled before assembly, and the carbine lubricated and hand operated, when assembly is complete, to test mechanisms.

d. The groups may be removed and disassembly accomplished with the tools provided and listed in SNL B-28.

e. Disassembly, assembly, and such repairs as may be handled by using arms personnel will be undertaken only under the supervision of an officer or the chief mechanic.

f. Disassembly of the following groups and parts are generally prohibited to the using arms:

(1) Magazine assembly.

(2) Barrel and receiver assembly.

(3) Barrel with gas cylinder assembly.

(4) Rear sight base.

DISASSEMBLY AND ASSEMBLY

(5) Front sight.

(6) Front band assembly.

(7) Recoil plate.

(8) Operating slide assembly.

(9) Stock and hand guard assemblies.

14. REMOVAL OF GROUPS. — *a. Barrel and receiver group.* — (1) Release magazine from the receiver by pressing magazine catch to left and withdrawing magazine downward, if it does not fall out.

(2) Retract bolt and glance into the chamber to insure that carbine is unloaded.

(3) Press sling swivel back against stock. Loosen front band by unscrewing front band screw part way *(Figure 6).* (The screw may be loosened with the head of a carbine cartridge). Press forward end of locking spring towards stock *(Figure 6)* and slide front band forward over front band locking spring. The front band cannot be removed from barrel until front sight is removed.

(4) Remove hand guard by sliding it forward on barrel until the liner is disengaged from undercut in the forward face of receiver, and then lifting it from barrel.

(5) Lift forward end of barrel and receiver group from stock (about 15°) until lug at rear end of receiver is disengaged from under retaining notch in face of recoil plate *(Figure 7).* When lug is clear, pull barrel and receiver forward and up and lift out of stock with trigger housing group attached.

b. Trigger housing group. — Push out trigger housing retaining pin from left side of forward end of trigger guard until clear of lug on receiver. Pull trigger housing forward until rear lug is clear of mating grooves in receiver, and then remove trigger housing group from receiver. Press retaining pin home in trigger housing to prevent loss. (See Figure 8, showing groups removed.)

c. Operating slide group (Figures 9 and 10). — (1) Draw operating slide spring guide slightly to rear until it is disengaged from operating slide, and then pull to right, and forward, and withdraw guide and spring from well in receiver. Disengagement of guide may be facilitated by retracting slide part way, then, holding spring and guide, push slide forward and remove guide as above.

(2) Draw operating slide slowly to rear until forward face of stop is in line with *forward* face of top of receiver. Pull handle up and to right until guide lug is free of retaining groove in receiver. Push body of slide forward until *rear* face of stop is in line with forward face of top of receiver and rotate slide body counterclockwise, freeing lug (by means of relief cut) from retaining guideways in barrel. Remove slide from barrel.

d. Bolt (Figures 11 and 12). — Grasp bolt by cam lug and slide to rear

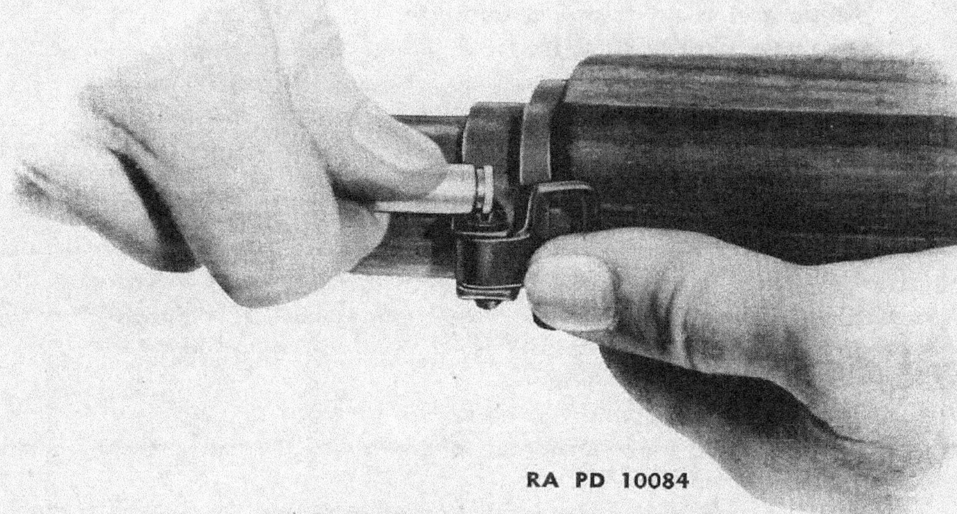

RA PD 10084

FIGURE 6A — REMOVING FRONT BAND SCREW

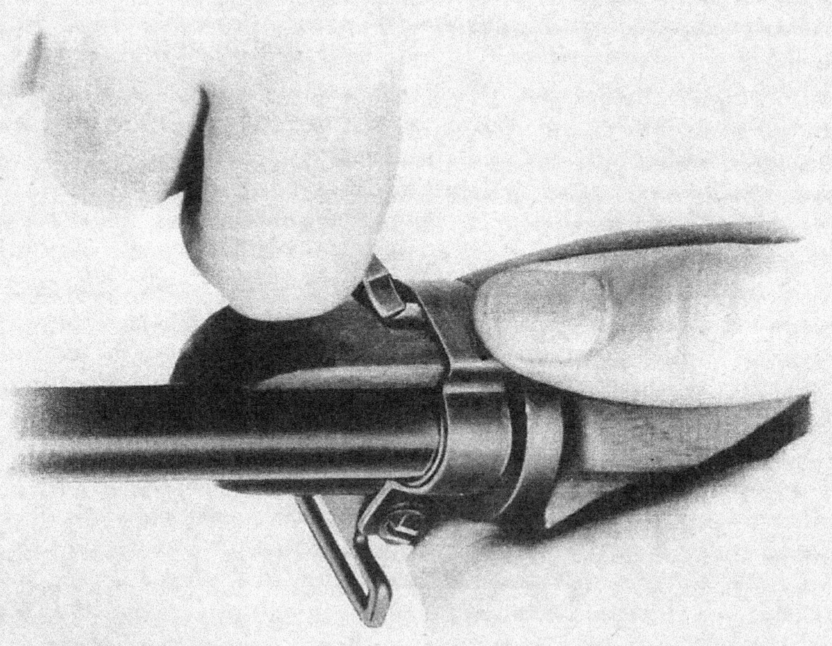

RA PD 10085

FIGURE 6B — DEPRESSING FRONT BAND LOCKING SPRING

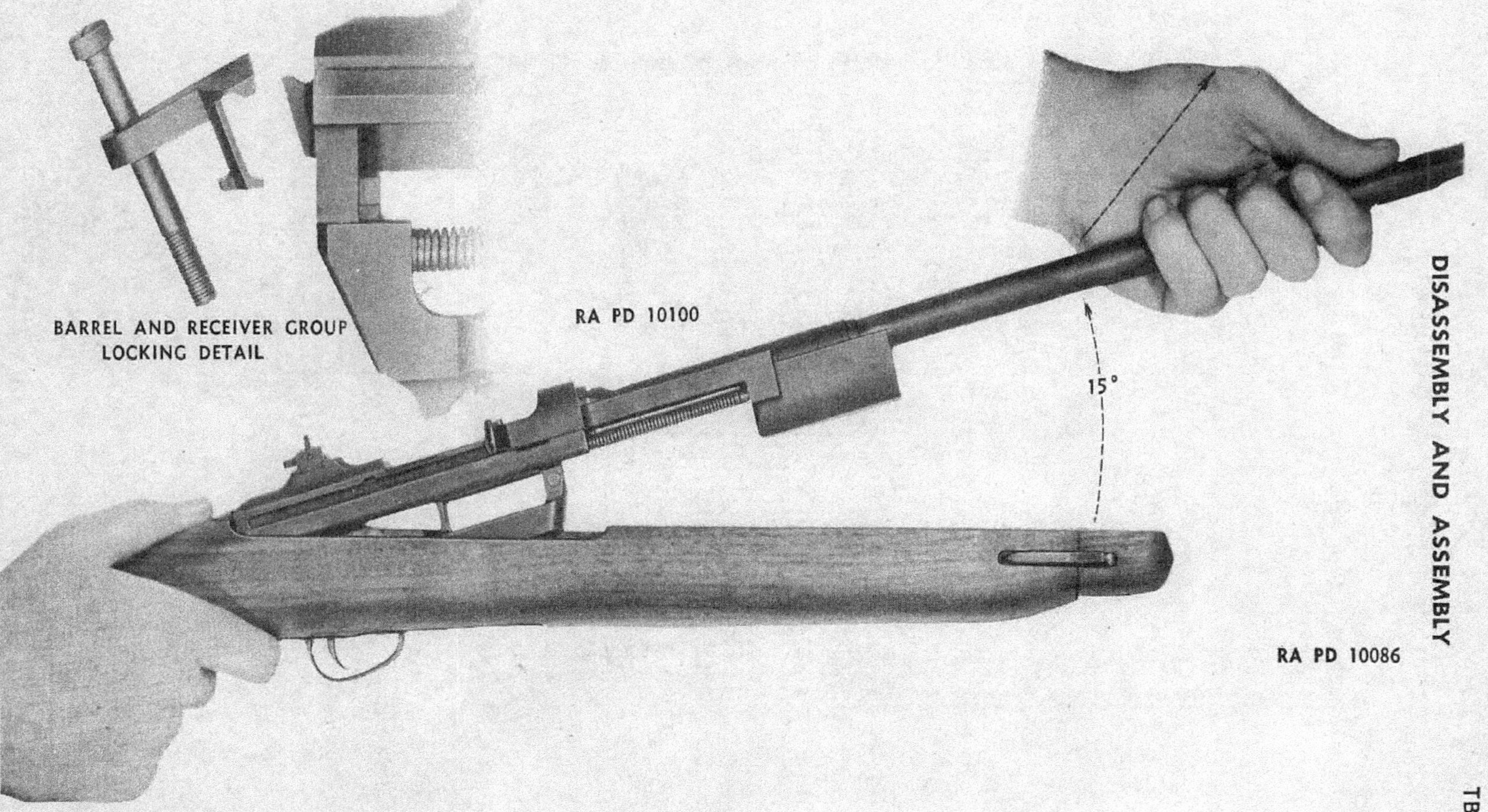

FIGURE 7 — REMOVING OR REPLACING BARREL AND RECEIVER GROUP FROM STOCK

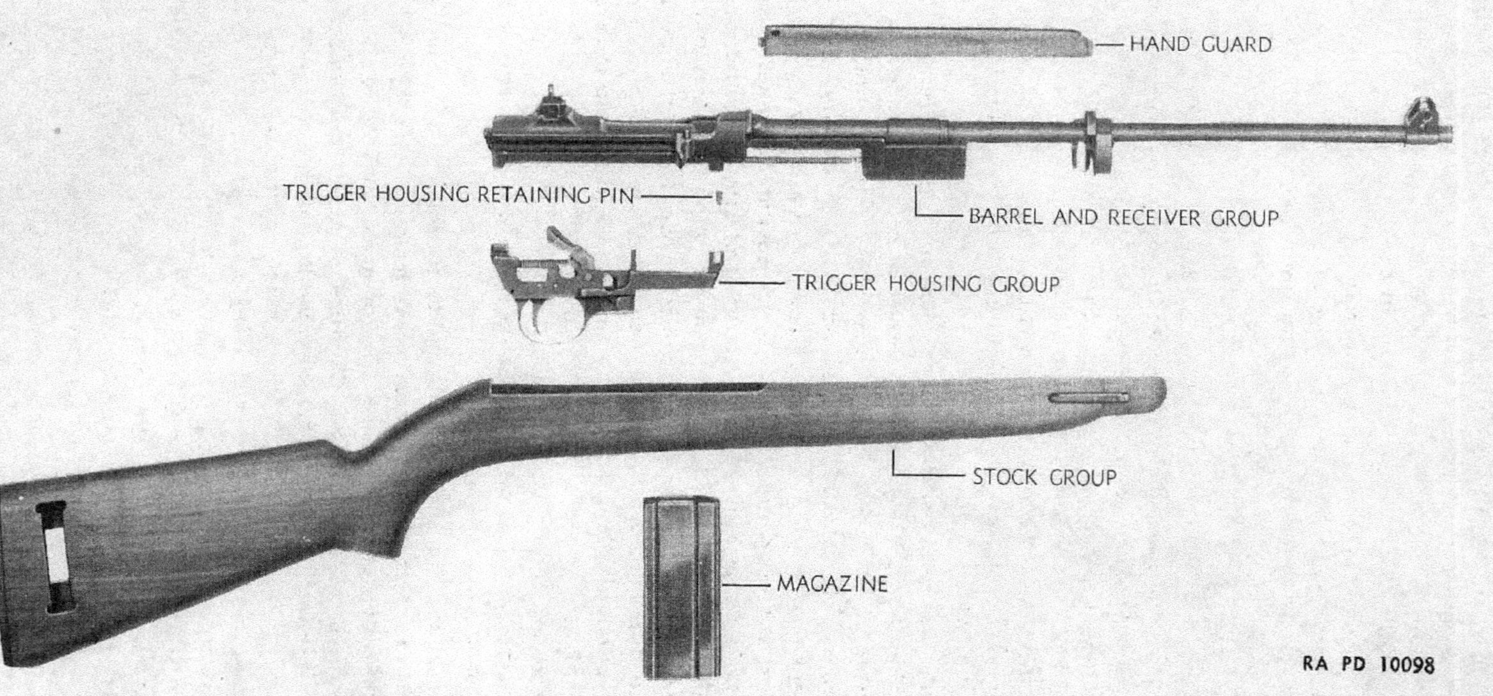

FIGURE 8 — GROUPS DISMOUNTED, SHOWING RELATIVE POSITION

DISASSEMBLY AND ASSEMBLY

until face of bolt is behind locking shoulder in receiver. Rotate bolt counterclockwise, lift up to angle of about 45°, and turn bottom up. Pull bolt forward and up, out of receiver. Bolt may be removed with trigger housing in position, but hammer must be in cocked position.

    e. Sling. — To remove sling, unbutton rear end of sling, withdraw from around oiler, and pull oiler to right out of aperture in stock. Unlock sling buckle and pull sling out of buckle and then out of sling swivel. Replace oiler in its loop in sling and rebutton sling, to prevent loss of parts.

    15. REPLACEMENT OF GROUPS. — *a. Bolt.* — With hammer cocked (trigger group assembled), grasp receiver in left hand and bolt in right, top down. Insert rear of bolt, at about 45° angle, into rear top of receiver, and then turn bolt top up, and cam lug facing up, at an angle of about 45°. Fit left guide lug of bolt in its groove in left side of receiver and then rotate bolt clockwise and slide forward. Bolt may be replaced with trigger housing in position, but hammer must be in cocked position.

    b. Operating slide group. — (1) With hammer cocked (trigger housing group assembled), hold body (forward end) of operating slide in the left hand and receiver in right. Place slide body against under side of barrel so that lug on right side is seated in its guideway, and lug on left side is opposite (mating with) relief cut in guideway in left side of barrel. Position bolt so that cam lug is in position to enter camming aperture in left side of slide handle. Start bolt cam lug into camming aperture in slide handle, and then rotate body of slide around barrel clockwise, until bolt lug fully enters camming aperture in slide handle and slide body lug enters relief cut in barrel. When lugs are so mated, push slide to rear until forward face of operating slide stop is level with forward face of rear top of receiver, and press operating slide handle in towards receiver so that lug on handle mates with relief cut in guideway on right side of receiver. Reciprocate slide to assure proper mating at both ends, and with bolt.

    (2) Place operating slide spring guide in spring, and free end of spring in well in forward face of receiver. Compress guide against spring and, with slide fully forward, insert nose of guide head into indentation in right rear face of slide body. Operate slide a few times to test assembly. Positioning of guide head may be facilitated by inserting rear end of spring and guide in well in receiver, then engage forward end of spring and rear face of operating slide and retract slide part way, compressing spring. Hold guide and spring in retracted position and move operating slide forward, then seat guide head as above.

    c. Trigger housing group. — With bolt in forward position and hammer cocked, place flat side of trigger housing flat upon under side of receiver with forward U-lug just ahead of lug on forward end of receiver. Slide

CARBINE, CAL. .30, M1

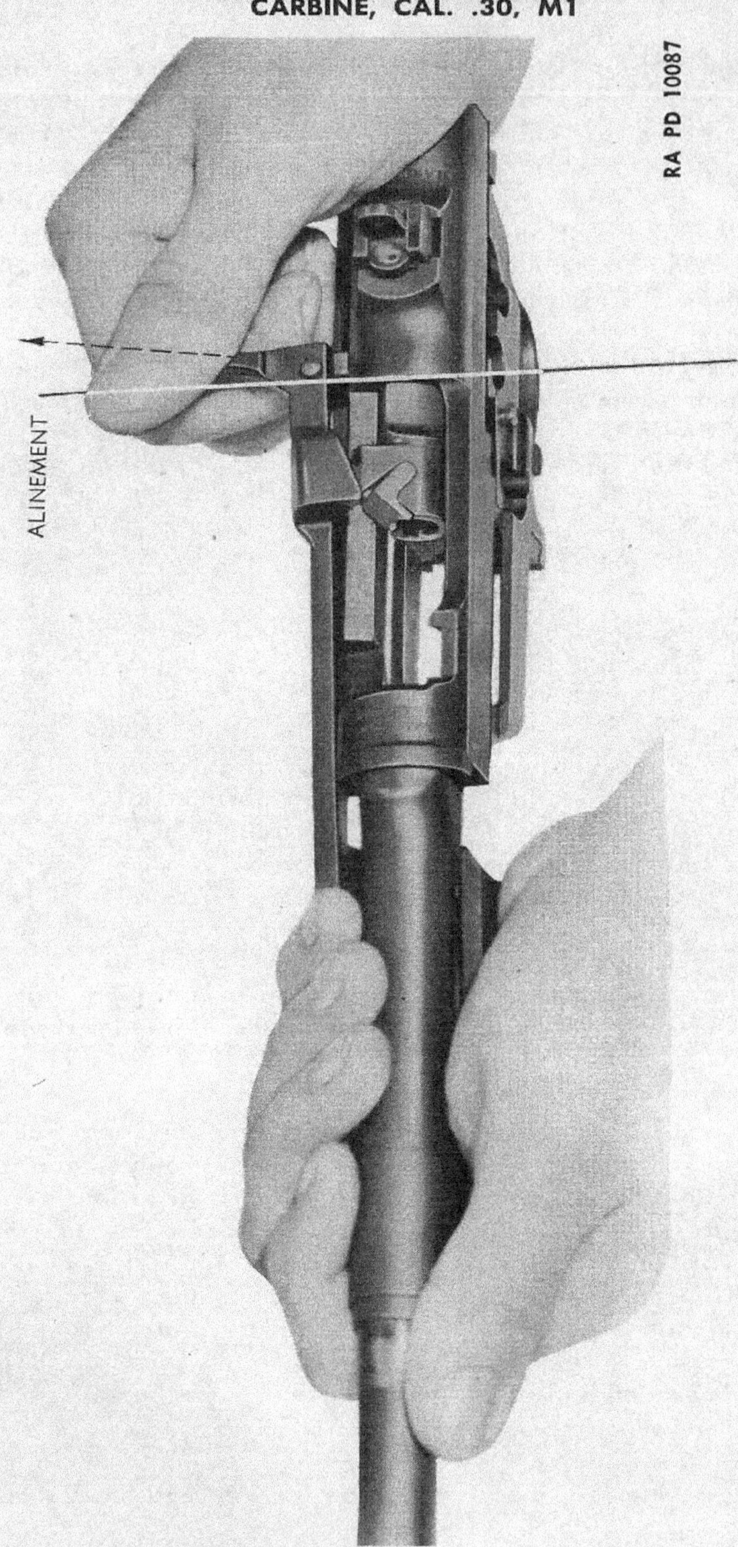

FIGURE 9 — REMOVING OPERATING SLIDE — FIRST MOVEMENT

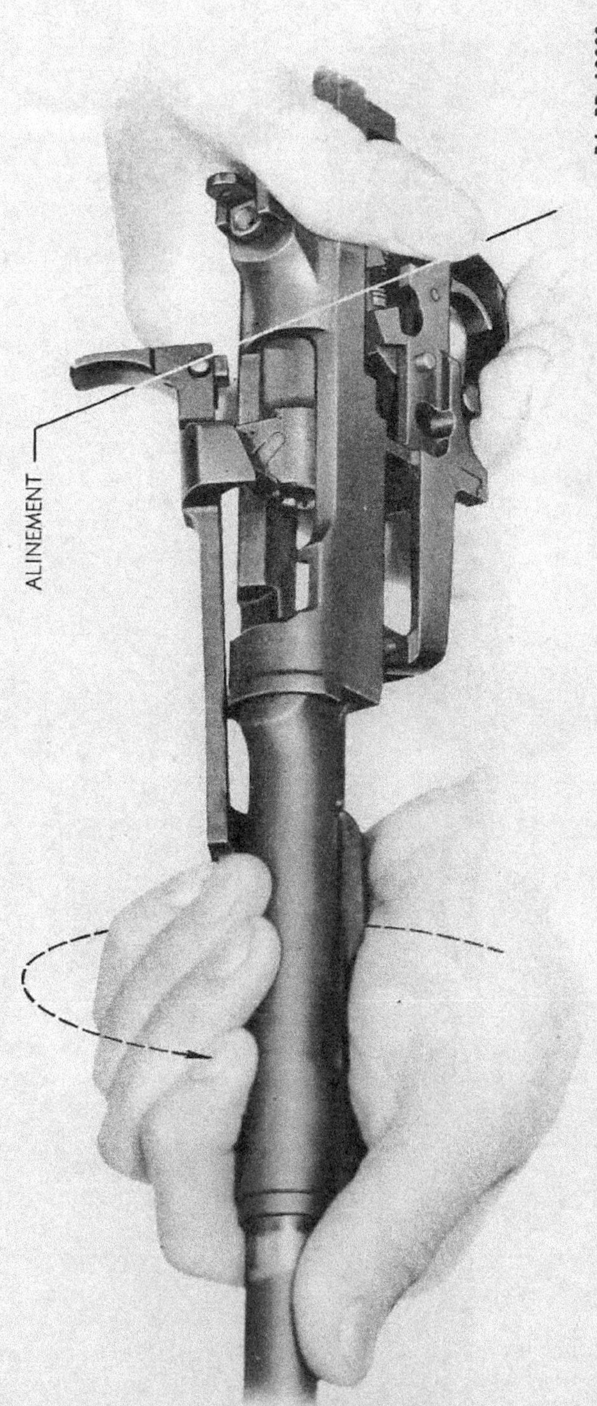

FIGURE 10 — REMOVING OPERATING SLIDE — SECOND MOVEMENT

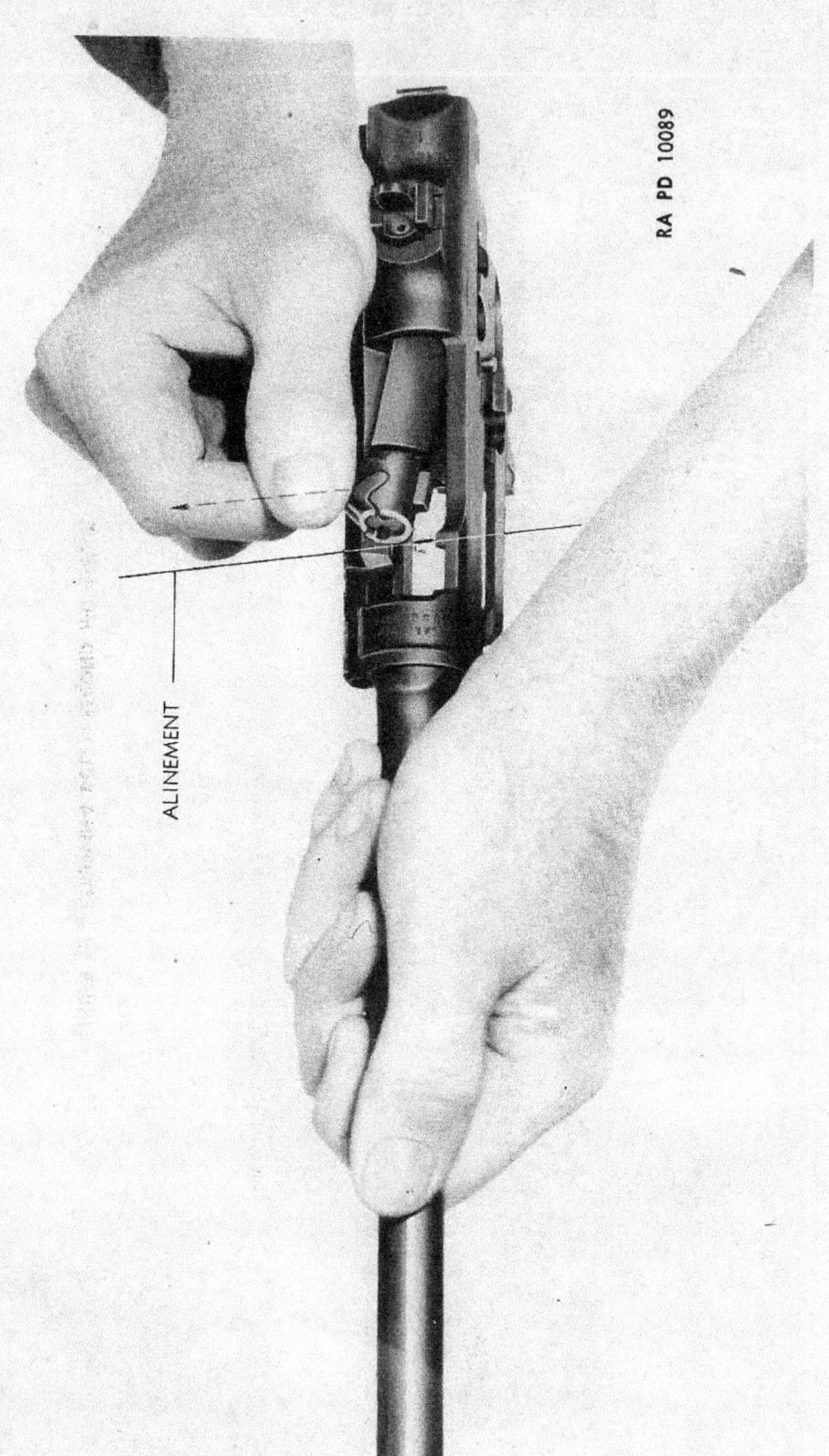

FIGURE 11 — REMOVING BOLT — FIRST MOVEMENT

DISASSEMBLY AND ASSEMBLY

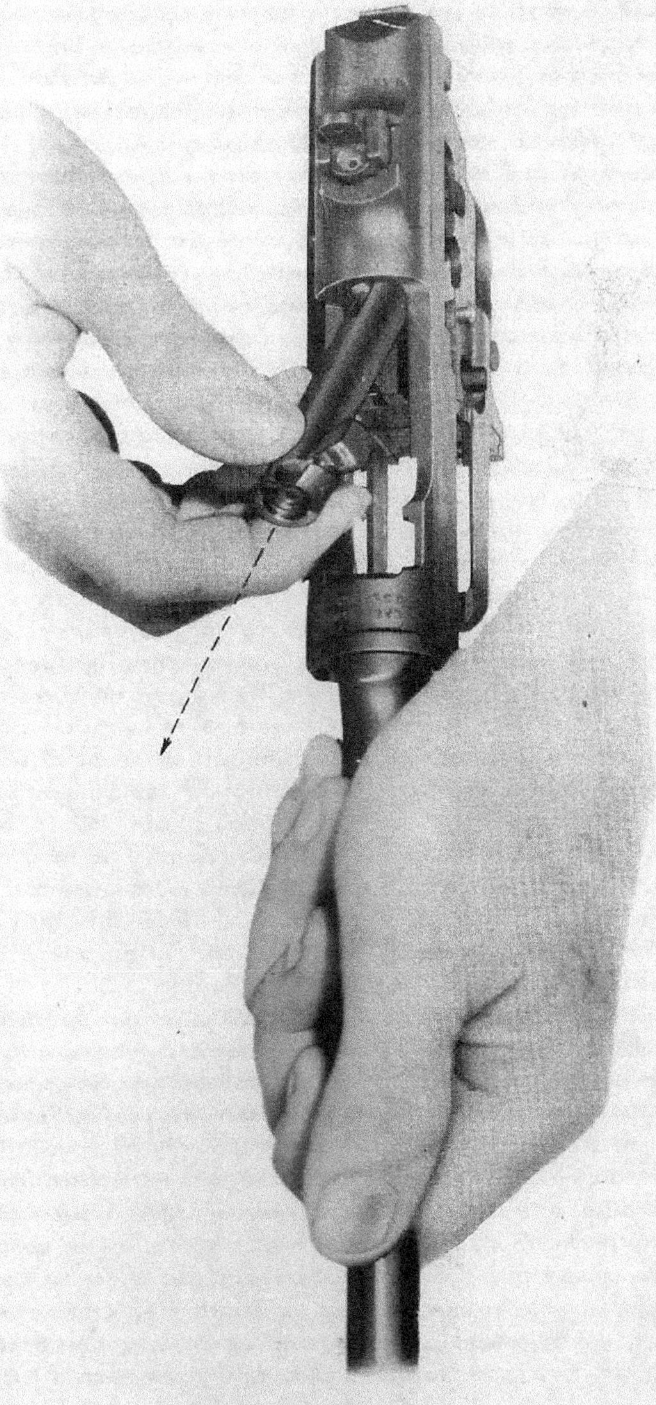

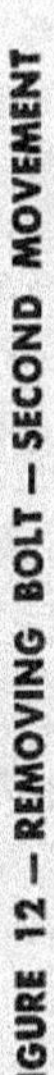

RA PD 10090

FIGURE 12 — REMOVING BOLT — SECOND MOVEMENT

CARBINE, CAL. .30, M1

housing to rear so that rear T-lug mates with and slides between L-lug on rear of receiver, and U-lug on forward end of trigger housing mate with lug on forward end of receiver. Aline pin holes in both forward lugs and insert trigger housing retaining pin from right side so that it is flush with both sides of U-lug. Be sure that trigger housing retaining pin spring is positioned in pin when inserting pin. Start pin (if fully withdrawn) into hole at slight angle so as to cam the spring into the hole.

d. Barrel and receiver group. — (1) Grasp stock in right hand and barrel and receiver group in left hand (by barrel). Insert trigger housing in aperture in top of stock and push back and down, with barrel at an angle of about 15°, until retaining lug on rear of receiver is beneath lip of retaining aperture in face of recoil plate, and back against rear face of recoil plate. Then slowly depress muzzle of barrel, at same time pressing to rear. If retaining lug does not cam up into aperture in recoil plate easily, *do not force,* but raise muzzle again and repeat operation until lug cams easily into aperture. Retaining aperture in recoil plate is an undercut, and retaining lug on rear of receiver has to cam into it after nose of lug is *behind* undercut. If pressure is exerted before this is accomplished, the great leverage obtained will injure the parts.

(2) When mating between lug and aperture is accomplished, lower barrel into bed in stock. Place hand guard flat on barrel and slide to rear so that metal liner mates with and enters retaining groove in forward face of receiver. Press hand guard fully home and slide front band over forward end of stock and hand guard, and press back, until behind front band locking spring. Seat evenly and tighten front band screw.

e. Sling. — Thread free (button) end of sling through sling swivel from the rear side and then through (unlocked) locking buckle. Place oiler in aperture in stock from right side, then thread button end of sling around oiler from rear to front. Mate button holes and insert button. To adjust sling, unlock buckle, pull sling through to desired length and relock buckle. (*See Figure 21,* showing early type sling. This sling has a friction type adjusting buckle and snap instead of a button).

16. MAGAZINE, DISASSEMBLY. (*Figure 13*). — Grasp magazine in left hand with base up and rounded face towards the body. With left thumb press up on forward (rounded) end of magazine base until the base can be slid to rear out of its retaining grooves in base of tube. Movement can be started by inserting rim of cartridge or similar instrument in recess in top of base. Remove magazine spring through opening thus obtained. Follower should not be removed unless necessary as tube may be sprung in process. To remove: position follower at bottom of tube. Insert screw driver or similar tool from top of tube to bear on rear end of follower and press on follower until stop flange is clear of tube. If flange will not rotate out, press *down* on opposite end to assist rotation. Do not force. Grasp flange and rotate follower out of tube.

DISASSEMBLY AND ASSEMBLY

NOTE: The magazine should not be disassembled except in emergency or for salvage.

17. MAGAZINE, ASSEMBLY. — Insert short (curved) end of follower into rear bottom (flat) side of magazine tube. Press down and rotate, until end of long side snaps under retaining flange. If necessary, insert screw driver or similar tool into top of tube to hold short end, and assist in rotation. Do not force unduly or magazine will be distorted. Push follower to top of tube and insert magazine spring with long side to the rear. (This permits the follower to slide easier in the tube.) Compress spring with thumb, and slide square end of base into retaining grooves in bottom of magazine until retained by projection on curved end slipping inside tube. Push follower down in tube and release to test smoothness of functioning. If follower does not slide up smoothly by spring action, tube has been distorted and should be corrected.

18. FRONT BAND, DISASSEMBLY. — Unscrew front band screw, remove it from band and remove swivel. There is no further disassembly of the band as the clip and piece are spot welded together. The front band cannot be removed from the barrel until the front sight is removed.

19. FRONT BAND, ASSEMBLY. — Place front band swivel between ends of front band piece with flat side facing forward and away from front band clip. Insert screw from top through piece and swivel and screw in part way. Do not tighten until band is assembled to stock and hand guard. If front band has been removed from the barrel it should be replaced so that the piece is towards the muzzle.

20. BARREL AND RECEIVER GROUP, DISASSEMBLY (Figure 14). — *a. Removing barrel from receiver.* — The barrel should not be removed from the receiver except for replacement. To remove, completely disassemble barrel and receiver. Wedge a hard wood block in receiver to prevent spring of the sides and clamp receiver in a vise having leather covered jaws. Position receiver in vise as near to barrel end as possible and clamp only tight enough to hold securely. Place strap wrench on barrel near receiver end and unscrew barrel anti-clockwise. (Barrel has right hand thread).

b. Front sight. — Do not remove unless necessary, as both ends of front sight blade pin are crimped into the body of the front sight blade and the front sight key is staked at the rear end into its keyway in the barrel. To remove sight from barrel, punch out front sight pin and drive sight forward from barrel, using hard wood block or brass drift. To remove key from barrel, tap lightly to rear to loosen staking, using hard wood block or brass drift, and lift key out of keyway.

c. Gas cylinder group. — (1) *Integral type.* — Unscrew piston nut from gas cylinder. Remove nut, elevate muzzle of barrel and slide piston out of gas cylinder. If piston will not slide out, tap cylinder lightly with wood

CARBINE, CAL. .30, M1

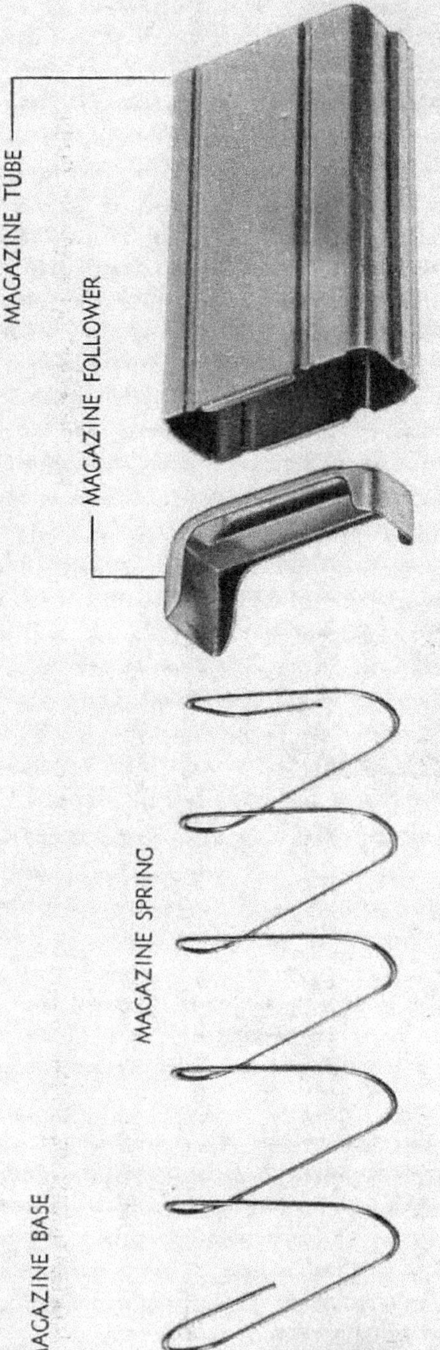

FIGURE 13 — MAGAZINE GROUP - EXPLODED VIEW

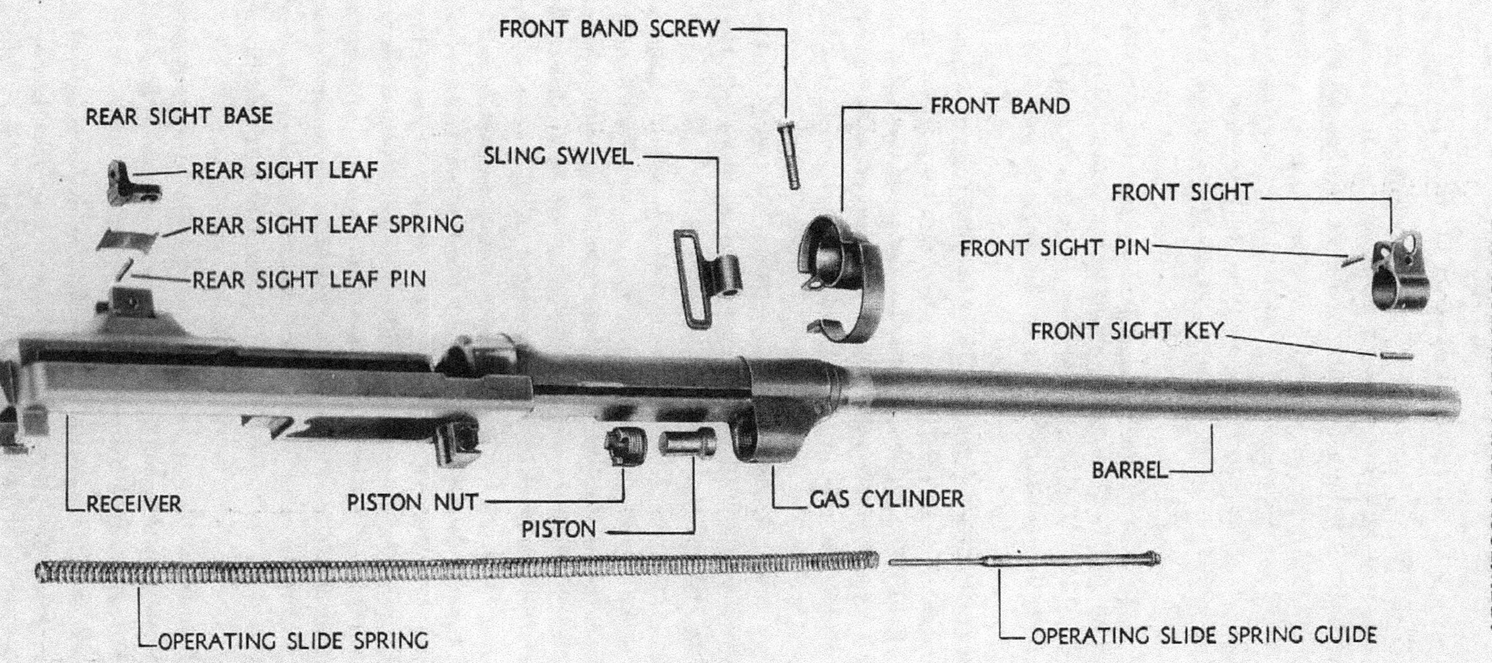

FIGURE 14 — BARREL AND RECEIVER GROUPS — EXPLODED VIEW

block. The integral type gas cylinder permits of no further disassemb[ly].

(2) *Removable type.* — Do not remove unless necessary for replaceme[nt]. Before removing, disassemble barrel and receiver and remove fr[ont] sight group as described in subparagraph *b* above. To remove gas c[yl]inder: remove piston nut and piston as in (1) above, punch out retaini[ng] pin, and drive gas cylinder forward off barrel, using hard wood blo[ck] or brass drift. When driving off, make contact with rear face of cylind[er] near barrel, so as to exert driving force as near parallel to barrel [as] possible.

d. Rear sight. — To disassemble rear sight group; spot a mark on re[ar] sight base and receiver for proper alinement upon assembly, drive o[ut] rear sight leaf pin and lift leaf and spring from sight base. Drive o[ut] base from right to left, using block of hard wood or brass drift (dov[e]tail tapers to right).

21. BARREL AND RECEIVER GROUP, ASSEMBLY. — *a. Replacing ba[r]rel in receiver.* — To assemble barrel to receiver, clamp receiver in vi[se] as described in paragraph 20 above. Start threading by hand and the[n] use strap wrench to screw barrel tightly into receiver. Screw barrel in[to] receiver (clockwise) tightly and turn until qualification marks on botto[m] of barrel and receiver are in line. Be careful to start threading correctl[y]. When assembled, flat lower surfaces of barrel and receiver should b[e] parallel, and extractor aperture in rear face of barrel should mate wi[th] extractor when bolt is locked.

b. Gas cylinder. — (1) *Integral type.* — Inspect gas cylinder and port f[or] foreign matter and wipe clean. Insert piston in gas cylinder, head firs[t] and screw piston nut in snugly allowing rear of piston to protrud[e] through nut. Shake barrel to be sure piston moves freely in gas cylinde[r] and protrudes sufficiently through nut (approx. ¼ inch).

(2) *Removable type.* — (a) The gas cylinder must be assembled to barr[el] before front sight is assembled. Slide gas cylinder on barrel with pisto[n] aperture on under side of barrel and facing to the rear. Aline flat side[s] of gas cylinder as closely as possible with flat sides of rear of barre[l] and drive cylinder on barrel, using block of hard wood or brass drif[t] until pin holes in cylinder and pin groove in barrel aline. Insert gas cy[l]inder pin and drive flush with both sides of cylinder.

(b) Assemble piston to gas cylinder as described in subparagrap[h] *b* (1) above.

NOTE: Gas cylinder is alined and drilled for pin, and gas port the[n] drilled upon manufacture. In assembling new gas cylinder to old barre[l] the alinement of gas port should be checked.

c. Front sight. — Place front sight key in keyway in top of barrel muzzl[e] with pin cut facing up. Tap key snugly to forward end of keyway, an[d] stake rear end of keyway to hold key in position. Slide front sight ont[o]

32

DISASSEMBLY AND ASSEMBLY

barrel with sloping faces of wings facing to rear. Mate keyway with key in barrel, and drive sight on barrel until pin hole in sight is in aline-ment with pin-cut in key. Insert pin and drive through until not quite flush with either side of sight. Stake metal over both ends of pin to hold in position.

    d. Rear sight group. — (1) If rear sight base has been removed, drive base into dovetail aperture in rear top of receiver from the left side (dovetail tapers to the right) until alining marks on sight base and receiver (made before disassembly) coincide. If no alining marks have been made, aline rear sight base so that center line of bore (chamber) and front sight blade aline midway between wings of rear sight base.

    (2) Position leaf spring between wings of base and press down leaf upon spring until pin holes in base and leaf aline. Insert rear sight leaf pin and drive flush. When leaf is in position, recessed face of aper-ture should face to front.

    22. TRIGGER HOUSING GROUP, DISASSEMBLY *(Figure 15).* — *a. Hammer group.* — (1) If hammer is not in forward position, pull trigger and ease hammer forward with the thumb.

    (2) Insert small punch or similar tool into hole in hammer spring guide and pull back until guide is clear of notch in hammer *(Figure 16);* then swing guide to right to clear hammer, and ease forward against force of spring until guide is clear of well in trigger housing. Pull guide from hammer spring. Punch out hammer pin and remove hammer.

    b. Trigger and sear group. — Pry up trigger spring until clear of seating slot in rear of trigger; then pull forward and up and remove from aper-ture in trigger housing. (Trigger spring may also be removed from the rear). Hold sear with thumb, against force of spring, and punch out trigger pin. Invert trigger housing and shake trigger and sear group from top of trigger housing. Pull sear spring from well in trigger.

    c. Magazine catch group. — Hold trigger housing bottom up in left hand, and with right hand insert small punch or similar tool into hole in lower face of trigger housing just forward of the bow *(Figure 16).* Engage punch ahead of magazine catch retainer plunger and pry plunger back from engagement with magazine catch. (Hold magazine catch with left thumb so that magazine catch spring and plunger do not fly out). Remove magazine catch and pull magazine catch plunger and spring out of trigger housing.

    d. Safety group. — Safety cannot be removed from trigger housing until magazine catch has been removed as described in c above. When mag-azine catch has been removed from trigger housing, safety spring and plunger and magazine catch retainer plunger may be removed through forward face of trigger housing, and safety pushed out of aperture. (Magazine catch retainer plunger and safety spring plunger are posi-tioned on opposite ends of the safety spring).

23. TRIGGER HOUSING GROUP, ASSEMBLY *(Figure 17).* — *a. Safety group.* — (1) Insert safety into its aperture ahead of trigger bow, with trigger cut·facing to rear.

(2) Assemble safety spring plunger and magazine catch retainer plunger to safety spring. Insert assembly into well in forward face of trigger housing (in magazine catch slideway). Operate safety sufficiently to see that safety spring plunger is engaged in aperture in forward face of safety.

b. Magazine catch group. — (1) Place magazine catch spring plunger in spring and spring in well in right side of trigger guard housing (just ahead of safety) with plunger facing out.

(2) Insert magazine catch into its guideway in forward face of trigger housing, from right side, with flange facing to rear, and press to left until stopped by retainer plunger. Depress retainer plunger into well in trigger housing and push catch to left until retaining plunger clicks into position to retain catch in guideway. Operate safety and catch a few times to test mechanism.

c. Trigger and sear group. — (1) Place trigger in trigger housing with long arm forward, and insert trigger pin part way to hold in position. Insert sear spring in well in body of trigger.

(2) Place sear in position in top of trigger, with long point facing forward and free end of sear spring seated in aperture in rear face of sear. Press sear back and down against force of spring until holes in trigger housing, trigger and sear are in line and then push trigger pin all the way through until flush with both sides of trigger housing.

(3) With trigger in *forward* position, insert trigger spring from the rear *(Figure 18)* into aperture in rear face of trigger housing so that loop of spring is down and forward, and push spring in until loop is stopped by rear of trigger. Pry up loop so that it slips into retaining slot in top rear face of trigger *(Figure 18)*. Operate trigger to test mechanism. (Trigger spring may also be replaced through forward end of aperture).

d. Hammer group. — (1) Position hammer in trigger housing with long end up and curving to rear. Engage sear notch with sear, and press lower part of hammer back and down until pin holes in trigger housing and hammer aline; then, insert hammer pin and position it so that there is an equal amount protruding from either side of the trigger housing. (A new type pin, with head, is provided to position the pin properly in the trigger housing. When assembling, push pin in up to shoulder.)

(2) Pull hammer slightly forward, retract trigger, and pull hammer to forward position. Insert hammer spring plunger into hammer spring. Hold free end of spring against face of trigger housing, central with hammer spring plunger recess, with plunger lying to right side of hammer.

(3) Insert small punch or similar tool into hole in hammer spring

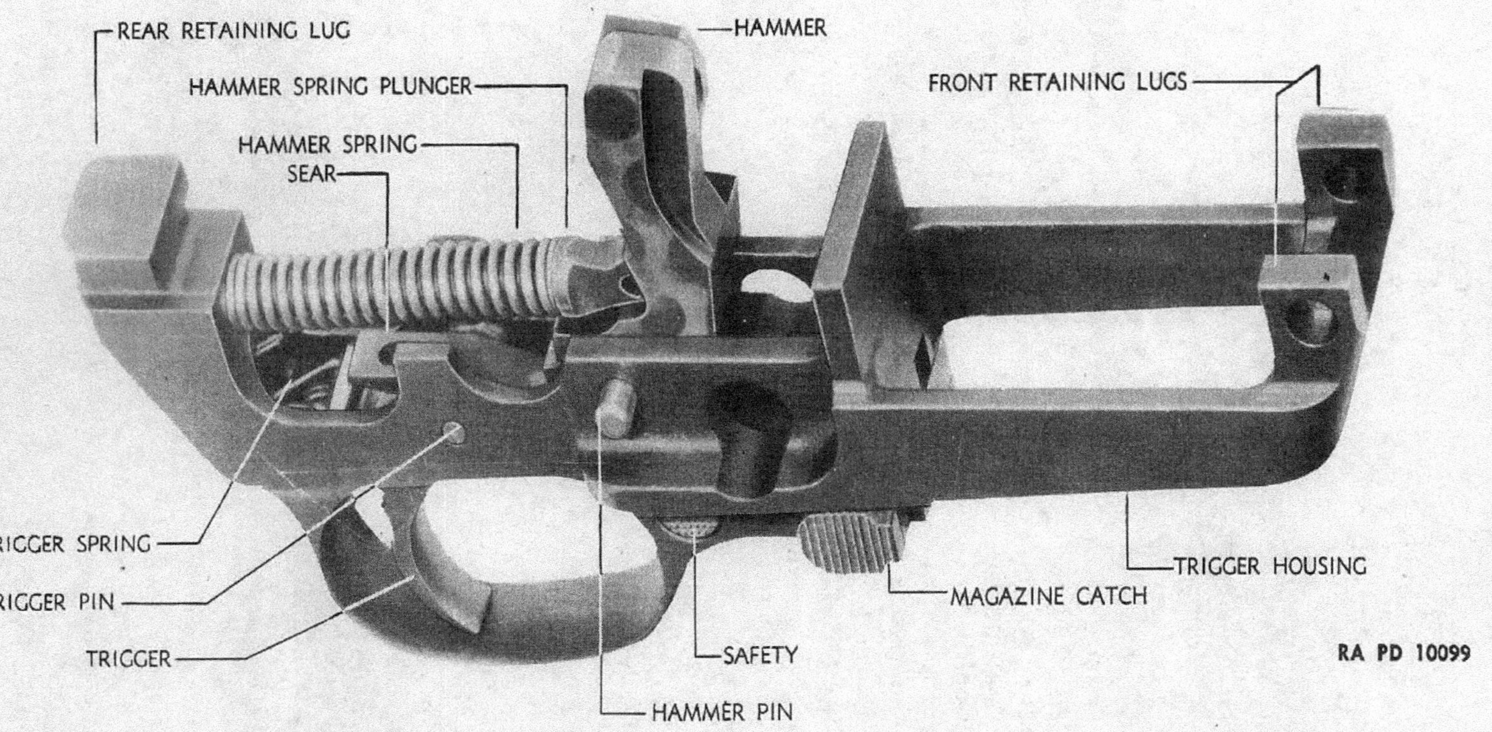

FIGURE 15 — TRIGGER HOUSING GROUP

CARBINE, CAL. .30, M1

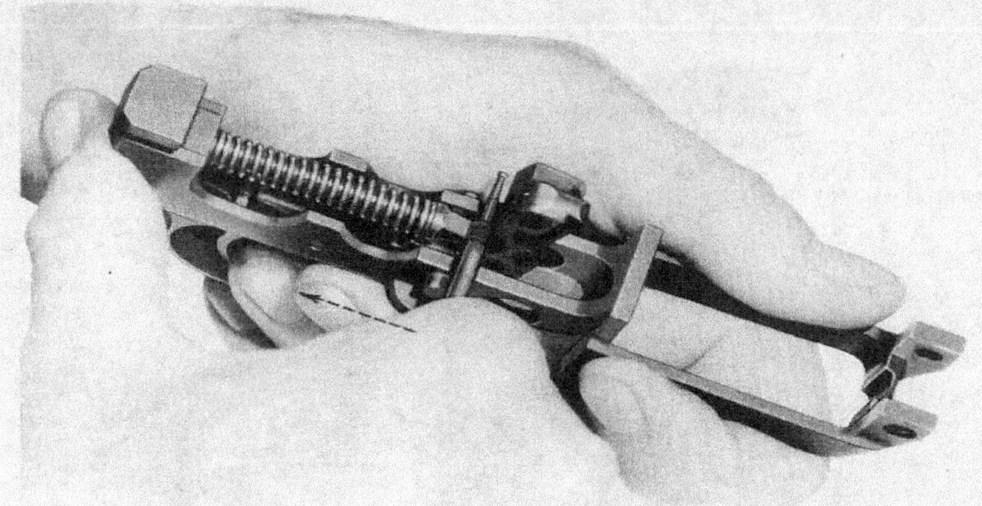

RA PD 10093

FIGURE 16A — DISENGAGING HAMMER SPRING PLUNGER

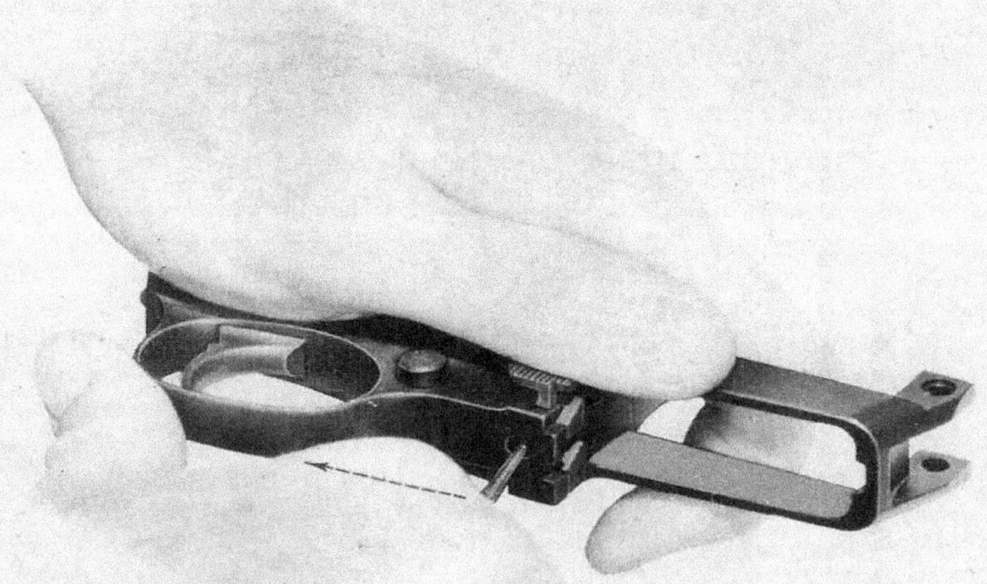

RA PD 10094

FIGURE 16B — DISENGAGING MAGAZINE CATCH RETAINER PLUNGER

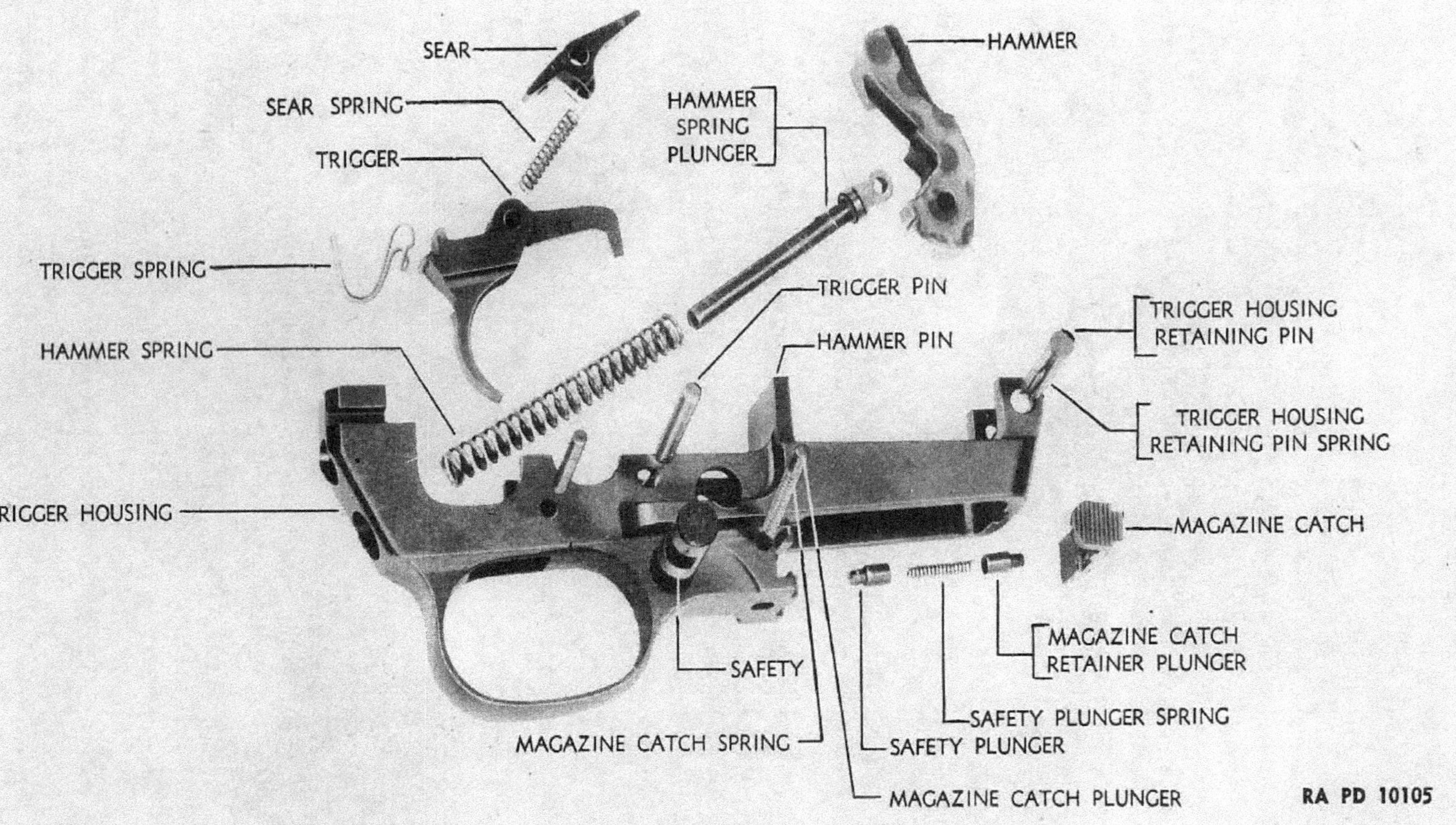

FIGURE 17 — TRIGGER HOUSING GROUP — EXPLODED VIEW

CARBINE, CAL. .30, M1

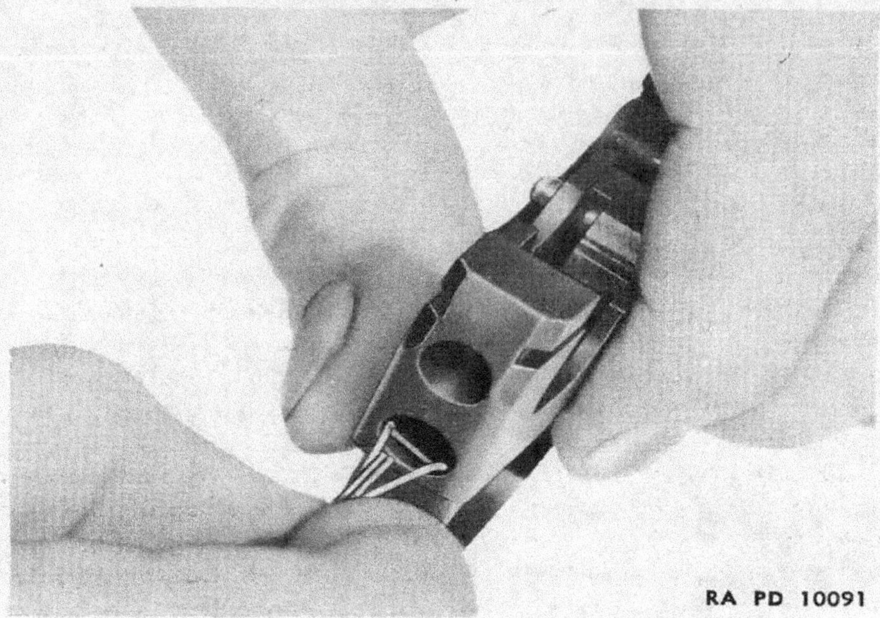

RA PD 10091

FIGURE 18A — INSERTING TRIGGER SPRING

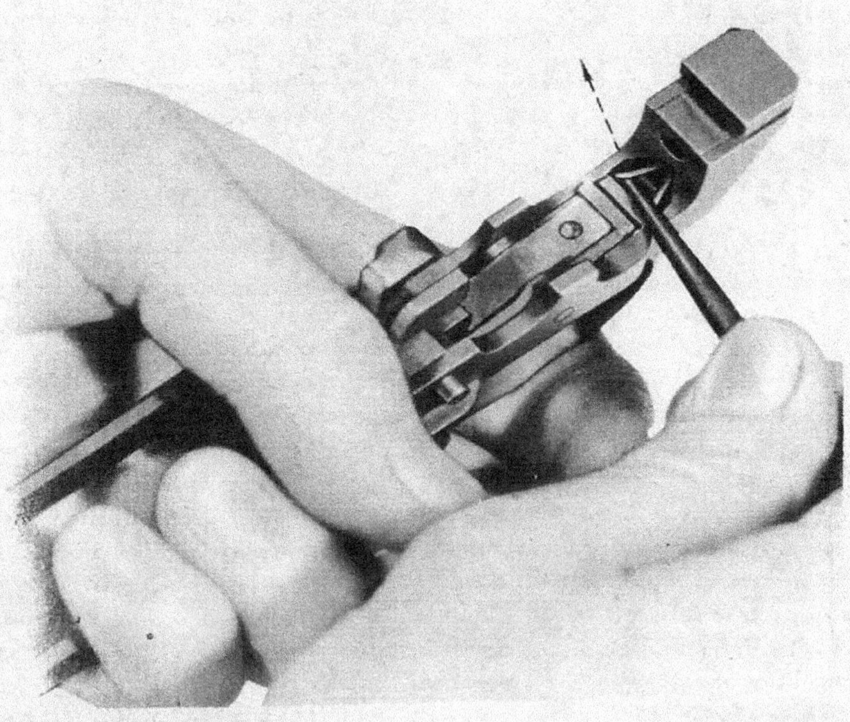

RA PD 10092

FIGURE 18B — SEATING TRIGGER SPRING

DISASSEMBLY AND ASSEMBLY

plunger and pull plunger back against force of spring, guiding rear end of plunger into recess in trigger housing. When forward end of plunger is even with rear face of hammer, press plunger to left and seat in retaining groove in base of hammer so that hole in plunger is horizontal.

(4) Operate assembled mechanism several times to test functioning.

NOTE: Alinement of plunger and aperture in trigger housing may be facilitated, during assembly, if spring and plunger are allowed to bear on top of the right lug protruding above the trigger pin.

24. OPERATING SLIDE GROUP, DISASSEMBLY (Figure 19). — The operating slide stop is the only removable part of the operating slide group. To remove operating slide stop, punch out retaining pin from right side. Be careful that stop and spring do not fly out when released. Lift stop and spring from well in operating slide.

25. OPERATING SLIDE GROUP, ASSEMBLY. — Assemble operating slide stop spring to stop and insert into aperture in top of slide handle with head of stop facing out. Depress stop against force of spring and insert retaining pin from left side, and drive flush. Operate stop to test functioning. (Nose of stop should protrude only when stop is pressed against force of spring).

26. BOLT GROUP, DISASSEMBLY (Figure 19). — The spindle of the extractor locks all other components of the bolt group into the bolt. To disassemble, hold thumb over face of bolt to prevent the ejector and extractor spring plunger from flying out when released, and punch the extractor out from the under side of bolt. Withdraw ejector and spring, extractor spring and plunger, and the firing pin from bolt.

27. BOLT GROUP, ASSEMBLY. — a. Insert firing pin into well in rear of bolt so that tang on rear of firing pin fits into aperture in rear end of bolt.

b. Assemble ejector spring to ejector so that it is locked in groove in ejector shank, and insert ejector assembly, spring first, into ejector well in lower front face of bolt.

c. Aline cut in firing pin with extractor spindle hole in bolt. Compress ejector in well and aline cut with that in firing pin and with extractor spindle hole. Insert hammer pin or similar pin into extractor spindle hole, from bottom, far enough to hold ejector and firing pin in place.

d. Assemble extractor plunger spring to extractor plunger and insert, spring first, into well in forward face of cam lug on right side of bolt.

e. Start extractor spindle into aperture hole in top of bolt and press extractor into aperture, camming extractor plunger back into its well. Continue to press extractor home until it pushes out the hammer (or holding) pin and seats in its aperture, flush with top of bolt. Test spring functioning of extractor and ejector.

28. STOCK AND HAND GUARD GROUP, DISASSEMBLY (Figure 20). — a. *Front band locking spring.* — Insert small, straight punch in spring

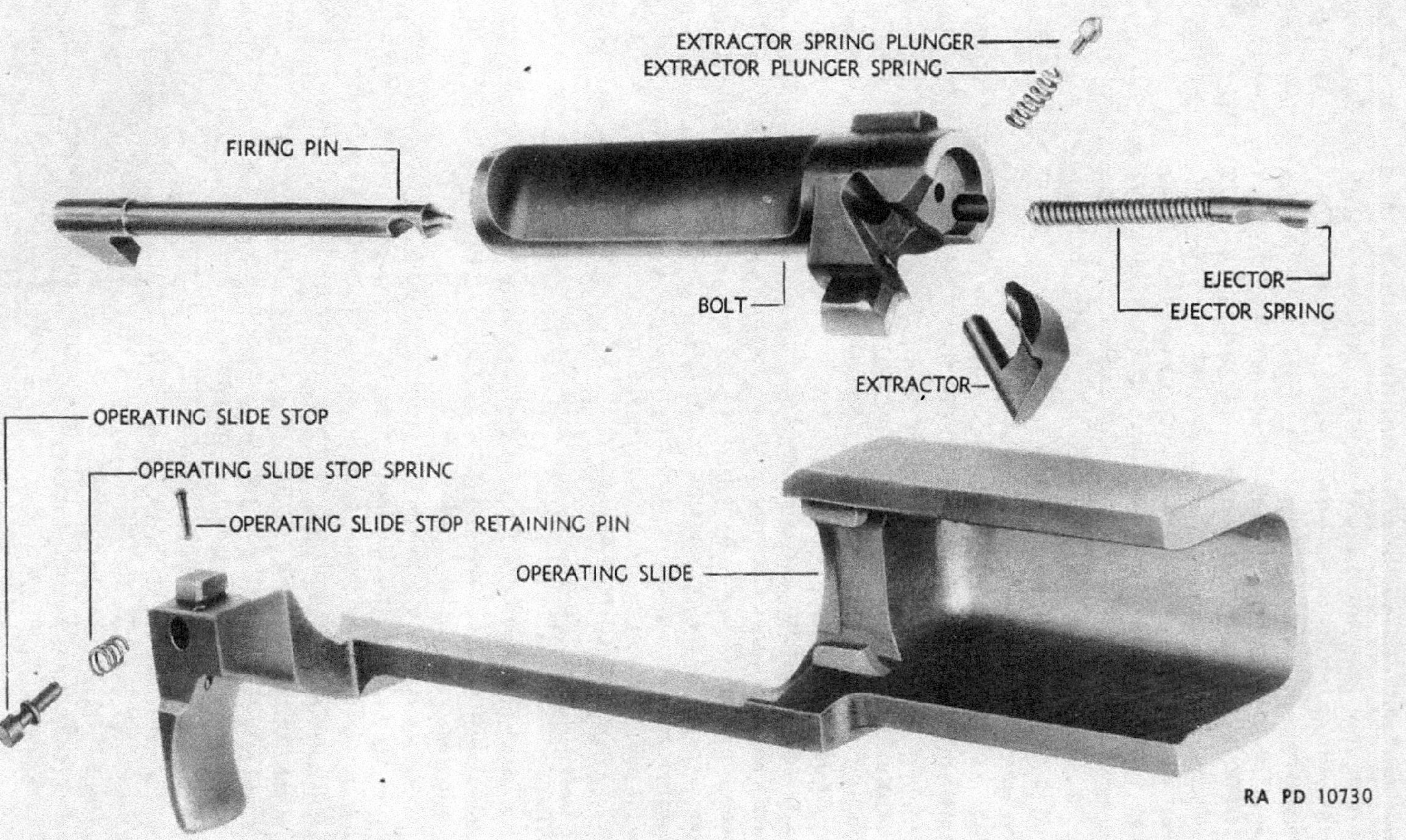

FIGURE 19 — BOLT AND OPERATING SLIDE GROUPS — EXPLODED VIEW

spindle hole in left side of forward end of stock and drive out front band locking spring (to the right) part way; spring may then be rotated and pulled from aperture.

b. Recoil plate. — (1) Unscrew recoil plate screw until clear of escutcheon threads (about ¾ inch), then withdraw from stock and recoil plate.

(2) Tap lightly on rear top face of recoil plate with a metal tool, and pull plate *directly forward* out of seating aperture in stock. Do not pull up or down, because rear seating lug on plate seats in a horizontal cut in the stock.

(3) The escutcheon should not be removed from the stock except for replacement. To remove, thread recoil plate screw all the way into escutcheon from the under side and pull escutcheon out of stock. If withdrawal is difficult, insert small straight punch from top of screw hole in stock and tap end of screw lightly to loosen escutcheon, or thread screw in from top, part way, and tap lightly, then proceed as above.

c. Butt plate. — Unscrew butt plate screw and remove from stock. Tap butt plate lightly with metal tool (to loosen) and pull to rear off stock. If butt plate is tight, do not pry off as stock is apt to be injured. Tap on edges lightly (all the way around) until loose enough to pull from stock.

d. Hand guard. — The liner of the hand guard assembly is riveted to the hand guard, and should not be removed except in emergency or for salvage. To remove, file off riveted head of rivets and punch out from the inside of hand guard.

29.   STOCK AND HAND GUARD GROUP, ASSEMBLY. — *a. Front band locking spring.* — Insert spindle of spring into hole in right forward end of stock, and drive to left. Seat spring fully in aperture in stock.

b. Recoil plate. — (1) Insert recoil plate into rear of receiver aperture in stock with bevel face up and tang to rear. Recoil plate must be inserted from front to rear and held level during insertion, so that seating lug and horizontal aperture mate. When in position, tap lightly to seat evenly and flush with stock.

(2) If escutcheon has been removed, insert small end first into aperture in under face of stock grip. Tap in until seated level and flush with stock. Replace recoil plate screw through top of recoil plate and stock, thread into escutcheon and draw down snugly.

c. Butt plate. — Place butt plate on butt and tap lightly until solidly and evenly seated on butt. Insert screw and turn down snugly. Do not force screw as threads in wood of stock may strip.

d. Hand guard. — If metal liner has been removed for replacement, position liner in rear face of hand guard so that it bears evenly on wood. Insert rivets from outside and rivet against metal liner. This should not be attempted without proper tools, or hand guard may be damaged. (Tubular rivets are used, which require a special riveter. In emergency, a spotting punch may be used).

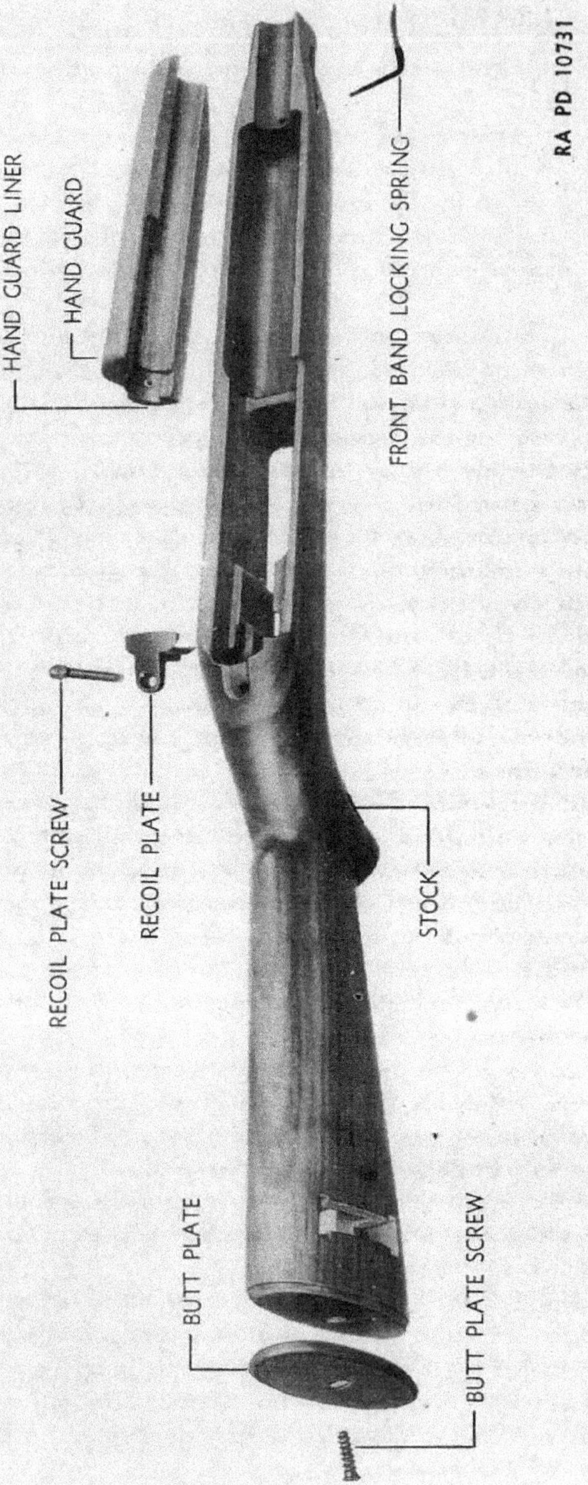

CARBINE, CAL. .30, M1

RA PD 10731

HAND GUARD LINER

HAND GUARD

FRONT BAND LOCKING SPRING

RECOIL PLATE SCREW

RECOIL PLATE

STOCK

BUTT PLATE

BUTT PLATE SCREW

FIGURE 20 — STOCK AND HAND GUARD GROUPS — EXPLODED VIEW

SECTION IV

CARE, CLEANING AND LUBRICATION

30. IN GARRISON AND CAMP. — *a.* Care and cleaning in garrison nd camp include the care of the carbine necessary to preserve its conition and appearance during the periods when no firing is being done. arbines in the hands of troops should be inspected daily to insure roper condition and cleanliness. Training schedules should allow roper time for cleaning carbines on each day when carbines are used training. For special care in extreme climates, refer to paragraphs and 37.

b. (1) The bore of the carbine will always be cleaned by inserting cleaning rod into the muzzle end. When cleaned, with carbine fully sembled, the bolt should be held in the open position by inserting a ece of wood between forward face of operating slide cam lug and ar right face of hand guard (or receiver). The operating slide stop is signed for holding the bolt in its rearmost position, but, if a cleaning d longer than the authorized one is used the end of the rod may ike the face of the bolt and release it. To protect the face of the bolt, piece of rag should be stuffed in the receiver. The magazine should be moved before cleaning the bore.

(2) To clean the bore, assemble a cloth patch to the cleaning rod d insert the rod into the bore at the muzzle end. Move it forward and ckward several times the entire length of bore and chamber and reace with a new patch. Repeat until a patch comes out clean. When ue patches are not available, patches should be cut to approximately inches square to permit their being forced through the bore without nding the cleaning rod. Then saturate a patch with the oil currently ed for lubrication and preservation of small arms and push it through bore, holding the carbine, top up, so that some of the oil will flow o the gas port. (OIL, lubricating, preservative, light, is a good prevative when available).

CAUTION: In cleaning the bore, care must be taken not to foul the aning patch in the gas port.

c. To clean the screw heads and crevices, use a small cleaning

brush or small stick. To clean the metal surfaces, wipe with a dry clc
to remove moisture, perspiration, and dirt, then wipe with a cloth cc
taining a small quantity of OIL, lubricating, preservative, light. This pi
tective film will be maintained *at all times.* To clean the outer wo
surfaces of the carbine, wipe off the dirt with a lightly oiled cloth a
clean with a soft dry one.

d. After cleaning and protecting the carbine as described abov
place it in the gun rack without covering and without a plug in t
muzzle or bore. Muzzle covers, gun covers, rack covers, and plugs mu
not be used because they cause sweating and promote rust. Howeve
when squad rooms are being swept, the gun racks may be covered
protect the carbines from dust. Covers must be removed after the roor
have been swept.

31. PREPARATORY TO FIRING. — Before firing, the following pr
cedure will be observed to assure the efficient functioning of the cc
bine. (Refer to paragraphs 36 and 37).

a. Dismount the main groups.

b. Remove all dirt and oil from bore and chamber with clec
patches.

c. Remove any carbon on the piston head and in the gas cylinde

d. Thoroughly clean and lightly oil all metal parts using OIL, lu
ricating, preservative, light.

e. *Do not oil the bore or chamber,* as hazardous chamber pressures m
develop. (See paragraph 51).

f. Lightly lubricate the following points, with a drop of oil fro
the oiler rod.

(1) Bolt lugs (locking and cam).

(2) Bolt guideways in receiver.

(3) Cocking cam on rear of bolt, and firing pin tang recess.

(4) Operating slide spring guide.

(5) Operating slide guideways in barrel.

(6) Operating slide (handle) guideway in receiver.

(7) Contacting surface of receiver and operating slide.

(8) Operating slide (handle) camming aperture.

(9) Piston shank.

CAUTION: Do not oil face or under side of bolt as oil may thus g
into chamber of the barrel.

g. A drop of oil should occasionally be placed on the operatir
slide stop, magazine catch and magazine catch retainer plunger, trigg
pin, hammer pin and hammer plunger.

h. Lubrication should be applied lightly, as too much oil collec
grit and foreign matter which will cause undue abrasive wear an
possible malfunction.

i. When bore and mechanism have been cleaned and oiled c

CARE, CLEANING AND LUBRICATION

described, assemble the carbine and rub all outer surfaces with a lightly oiled rag.

32. AFTER FIRING. — The bores of all carbines must be thoroughly cleaned by the evening of the day on which they are fired. They should be cleaned in the same manner for the next 3 days. (Refer to paragraphs 36 and 37).

CAUTION: Under no circumstances will metal fouling solution be used in this carbine.

a. Immediate cleaning after firing, or as soon as possible. — Hold the carbine bottom side up, so that no cleaning fluid (or water) will enter the gas port in the bore. Run several patches saturated with CLEANER, rifle bore, through the bore. If rifle bore cleaner is not available, warm soapy water (issue soap) or warm water alone should be used. Remove patch from cleaning rod and assemble the cleaning brush to the rod end. Run brush back and forth through the bore several times while the bore is still wet. Care should be taken to insure that the brush goes all the way through the bore before the direction is reversed, and that the chamber is thoroughly cleaned its entire length. The diameter of the chamber in the carbine is so near that of the bore, that additional cleaning should not be, as a rule, necessary. After using the brush, run several wet patches through bore and chamber, removing them from the breech end. Follow this by dry, clean patches until patches come out clean and dry. Saturate a patch in OIL, lubricating, preservative, light, and push it through the bore and chamber, holding the carbine, top side up, so that some of the oil will flow into the gas port in the bore.

CAUTION: In cleaning the bore, care must be taken not to foul the cleaning patch in the gas port.

b. Complete cleaning. — This cleaning should be done with the groups dismounted, and as soon as possible after that described in subparagraph *a* above. If the carbine is to be fired the next day, proceed as, in paragraph 31. If the carbine is not to be fired in the next few days, repeat procedure in subparagraph *a* above for 3 days. In addition, the following instructions will be observed:

(1) *Gas cylinder and piston.* — After extensive firing, remove the piston nut from the gas cylinder and remove the piston. Clean out all excess carbon from gas cylinder and from head of piston. Care should be used when removing carbon not to scratch gas cylinder or piston unnecessarily. Check gas port in barrel after cleaning to make sure it is free, and test piston for freedom of action in gas cylinder and through piston nut when reassembled. In rearward position, piston should protrude about ¼ inch.

(2) *Exterior surfaces.* — Wipe off the exterior of the carbine with a dry cloth to remove dampness, dirt, and perspiration. Wipe all metal surfaces with OIL, lubricating, preservative, light, and the stock and hand

guard with OIL, linseed, raw.

33. ON THE RANGE OR IN THE FIELD. — The carbine must be kep clean and free from dirt and properly lubricated with lubricating oil To obtain its maximum efficiency the following points must be observed (Refer to paragraphs 36 and 37).

a. Never fire a carbine with any dust, dirt, mud, or snow in the bore.

b. Keep the chamber clean and free from oil and dirt.

c. Never leave a patch, plug, or other obstruction in the chamber or bore. Neglect of this precaution may result in serious injury.

d. If the carbine gives indications of lack of lubrication and excessive friction, apply additional lubricating oil to the parts listed in paragraph 31 *f.* Excessive friction exists if the empty cases are being ejected to the right rear, and oil should be applied at the first opportunity as failures to feed and eject will occur if the condition is not corrected.

e. Keep a light coating of oil on all other metal parts.

f. Remove the carbon from the gas cylinder and the piston head when necessary. (Sluggish action of carbine may indicate clogged piston).

g. In general, it should not be necessary to remove any of the parts of the carbine in the field for cleaning, except to dismount the barrel, receiver and trigger housing group from the stock. Due to position of gas port, the gas cylinder and piston should not require cleaning often. However, if the mechanism becomes very dirty, the part groups may be removed from the carbine (paragraph 14) and the necessary cleaning and lubrication accomplished.

h. During range firing, a selected and qualified man should be placed in charge of the cleaning of carbines at the cleaning racks or tables.

34. PREPARATION OF CARBINES FOR STORAGE. — *a.* OIL, lubricating, preservative, light, is the most suitable oil for preserving the mechanism of carbines. This oil is efficient for preserving the polished surfaces, the bore, and the chamber for a period of from 2 to 6 weeks, dependent on the climatic and storage conditions. Carbines in short term storage should be inspected every five days and the preservative film renewed if necessary.

b. COMPOUND, rust preventive, light, is a semisolid material. This compound is efficient for preserving the polished (metal) surfaces, the bore, and the chamber for a period of 1 year or less, dependent on the climatic and storage conditions.

c. The carbines should be cleaned and prepared with particular care. The bore, all parts of the mechanism, and the exterior of the carbines should be thoroughly cleaned and then dried completely with rags. In damp climates, particular care must be taken to see that the rags are

CARE, CLEANING AND LUBRICATION

dry. After drying a metal part, the bare hands should not touch that part. All metal parts should then be coated either with OIL, lubricating, preservative, light, or rust preventive compound, depending on the length of storage. (See a and b above). Application of the rust preventive compound to the bore of the carbine is best done by dipping the cleaning brush in rust preventive compound and running it through the bore two or three times. (Cleaning brush must be clean). Before placing the carbine in the packing chest see that the bolt is in its forward position and that the hammer is released. Then, handling the carbine by the stock and hand guard only, it should be placed in the packing chest, the wooden supports at the butt and muzzle having previously been painted with rust preventive compound. Under no circumstances should a carbine be placed in storage contained in a cloth or other cover or with a plug in the bore. Such articles collect moisture which causes the weapon to rust.

35. CLEANING OF CARBINES AS RECEIVED FROM STORAGE. — a. Carbines which have been stored in accordance with paragraph 34 will be coated with either OIL, lubricating, preservative, light, or COMPOUND, rust preventive, light. Carbines received from ordnance storage will, in general, be coated with heavy rust preventive compound. Use a light oil or SOLVENT, dry cleaning, to remove all traces of the compound, or oil, particular care being taken that all recesses in which springs or plungers operate are cleaned thoroughly. After using the dry cleaning solvent, make sure it is completely removed from all parts. Then follow instructions contained in paragraph 30. If the carbine is to be fired immediately, follow instructions contained in paragraph 31.

NOTE: Failure to clean the firing pin and the recess in the bolt in which it operates may result in gun failure at normal temperatures, and will most certainly result in serious malfunctions if the carbines are operated in low temperature areas, as rust preventive compound and other foreign matter will cause the lubricating oil to congeal or frost on the mechanism.

b. Dry cleaning solvent is a petroleum distillate, of low inflammability and noncorrosive, used for removing grease. It is generally applied with rag swabs to large parts and as a bath for small parts. The surfaces must be thoroughly dried immediately after removal of the solvent. To avoid leaving finger marks, which are ordinarily acid and induce corrosion, gloves should be worn by persons handling parts after such cleaning. Dry cleaning solvent will attack and discolor rubber.

36. CARE AND CLEANING IN COLD CLIMATES. — a. In temperatures below freezing, it is necessary that the moving parts of the carbine be kept absolutely free from moisture. It has also been found that excess oil on the working parts will solidify to such an extent as to cause sluggish operation or complete failure.

b. The metal parts of the carbine should be taken apart and completely cleaned with SOLVENT, dry cleaning, before use in temperatures below 0°F. The working surfaces of parts which show signs of wear may be lubricated by rubbing with an oiled cloth. At temperatures above 0°F, the carbine may be oiled lightly after cleaning by wiping with a slightly oiled cloth, using OIL, lubricating, preservative, light.

c. (1) Immediately upon bringing indoors, the carbine should be thoroughly oiled, using OIL, lubricating, preservative, light, because moisture condensing on the cold metal in a warm room will cause rusting. After the carbine has reached room temperature, it should be wiped free of condensed water vapor and oiled again.

(2) If carbine has been fired, it should be thoroughly cleaned and oiled. The bore may be swabbed out with an oily patch and when the weapon reaches room temperature, thoroughly cleaned and oiled as prescribed in paragraph 32.

(3) Before firing, the carbine should be cleaned and oil removed as prescribed in paragraph *b* above. The bore and chamber should be entirely free of oil before firing.

37. CARE AND CLEANING IN HOT CLIMATES. — *a. Tropical climates.*

(1) In tropical climates where temperature and humidity are high, or where salt air is present, and during rainy seasons, the carbine should be thoroughly inspected at frequent intervals and kept lightly oiled when not in use. The groups should be dismounted at regular intervals and, if necessary, disassembled sufficiently to enable the drying and oiling of parts.

(2) Care should be exercised to see that unexposed parts and surfaces are kept clean and oiled, such as the under side of the barrel, recoil plate recess, gas cylinder, piston, spring wells and like parts and surfaces.

(3) In hot climates, OIL, lubricating, preservative, light, should be used for lubrication.

(4) Wood parts should also be inspected to see that swelling due to moisture does not bind working parts. (In such cases shave off wood *only enough* to relieve binding). A light coat of OIL, linseed, raw, applied at intervals and well rubbed in, with the heel of the hand, will help to keep moisture out. Allow oil to soak in for a few hours and then wipe and polish wood with dry clean rag.

NOTE: Care should be taken that linseed oil does not get into mechanism or on metal parts as it will gum up when dry. Stock and hand guard should be dismounted when oil is applied.

b. Hot, dry climates. — (1) In hot dry climates where sand and dust are apt to get into the mechanism and bore, the carbine should be wiped clean daily or oftener if necessary. Groups should be dismounted and disassembled as far as necessary to facilitate thorough cleaning.

CARE, CLEANING AND LUBRICATION

(2) Oiling and lubrication should be kept to a minimum, as oil will collect dust which will act as an abrasive on the working parts and foul the bore and chamber. OIL, lubricating, preservative, light, is best for lubrication where temperatures are high, and should be lightly applied only to the surfaces of working parts showing signs of wear.

(3) In such climates, wood parts are apt to dry out and shrink, and a *light* application of raw linseed oil, applied as in subparagraph *a* (4) above, will help to keep wood in condition.

(4) Perspiration from the hands is a contributing factor to rust on account of acid present in perspiration, and metal parts should be wiped dry frequently.

(5) During sand or dust storms, breech and muzzle should be kept covered if possible.

38. FIELD INSPECTION. — The carbine should be inspected at intervals for operation and functioning. In such inspections, dummy cartridges should be used if available; use of live ammunition is prohibited.

a. With dummy cartridges in the magazine, retract and release the operating slide, to load and eject the dummy cartridges. During the operation check the following points:

(1) Smooth functioning of operating slide and bolt; they should reciprocate smoothly and easily, without undue looseness.

(2) Complete locking of bolt, and continued forward movement of the operating slide; the slide should continue to move forward about 5/16 inch after the bolt is fully locked.

(3) Grip of extractor on cartridge and action of ejector; extractor should grip base of cartridge firmly and ejector throw it off the bolt as soon as cartridge is clear of receiver; if cartridge is not extracted or is carried to rear before ejection, extractor claw may be damaged, extractor plunger or spring broken or missing, or ejector spring weak or broken.

(4) Position of cartridge in mouth of magazine; magazine follower should position cartridge in line with bolt and fully up against lips of magazine. If otherwise, magazine spring may be weak or tube or follower dented or burred.

(5) Engagement of sear with hammer; sear should engage with sear notch in hammer when bolt is about half way retracted. A distinct click may be heard as sear slides forward into the sear notch in hammer under force of sear spring. The bolt should always be fully retracted to insure complete engagement and retention of sear. If click is not heard or trigger pull appears to be light or excessively heavy, the sear and sear notch in hammer should be examined for burs, foreign matter in the sear notch or weak or broken sear spring. Trigger pull should not be under 4 pounds nor over 6 pounds.

CARBINE, CAL. .30, M1

b. Functioning of the parts given below should be checked as indicated.

(1) *Bolt.* — With operating slide assembled to bolt, and spring and guide disassembled from slide, reciprocate bolt by means of the operating slide handle. The bolt and slide should move freely in their guideways. The bolt will check slightly (with hammer cocked) as it rides over the hammer on its rearward movement. If binding of bolt and slide is apparent, disengage slide from bolt and operate individually to ascertain point of binding. Burs may occur in bolt, or operating slide guideways, on bolt locking shoulders in receiver, lugs of bolt or operating slide. Such burs should be removed (stoned to a polish) with a fine grained sharpening stone.

(2) *Trigger.* — Trigger should move forward under force of trigger spring when released from rearward position. If trigger does not move forward positively, trigger spring may be broken, disengaged, or bent.

(3) *Safety.* — Safety should block trigger when pushed fully to right and release trigger when pushed fully to left.

(4) *Magazine catch.* — Magazine catch should return to position smartly when released after it is pressed to left to disengage from magazine. If action is sluggish, examine for burs, foreign matter or lack of lubrication.

(5) *Front band.* — Front band should be secure at all times, with screw drawn down snugly and locking spring engaged positively with front band lying behind nose of locking spring. If spring will not depress, look for foreign matter in stock aperture. If spring does not engage positively with front band, look for bent spring.

(6) *Rear sight.* — Force of rear sight leaf spring should hold one segment of leaf upright at all times. If spring action is not positive, spring may be broken or foreign matter present under leaf or spring.

(7) *Recoil plate.* — Recoil plate should be snugly seated in its aperture and screw drawn down tightly. Looseness of recoil plate or receiver retaining lug in plate aperture will cause barrel and receiver group to become loose and eventually damage stock and/or receiver. Burs arising from improper positioning of lug in plate, when assembling, should be peened down before stoning so as not to reduce metal on lug.

(8) *Piston.* — Piston may reciprocate sluggishly due to excess carbon on piston head or in gas cylinder. Piston should reciprocate in gas cylinder and through piston nut (about ¼ inch) when barrel is shaken. The piston nut should be kept tight at all times.

NOTE: If piston becomes "frozen" in gas cylinder, due to rust or carbon, soak with penetrating oil for about one hour, and then work loose and shake out. Loosening may be helped by working with a prick punch or similar tool through gas port hole in outside of gas cylinder. When removed, piston and gas cylinder should be thoroughly cleaned, oiled and examined for burs, and gas port examined for foreign matter.

(9) *Operating slide spring guide.* — Operating slide spring and guide should work freely in well in receiver. If binding is apparent, look for bent guide or foreign matter in well.

(10) *Operating slide.* — Operating slide should not become disengaged from receiver when reciprocated. If this happens, look for bent handle or excessively worn retaining lugs on operating slide body.

(11) *Operating slide stop.* — Operating slide stop is for the purpose of "hanging" the bolt in the open position. If stop spring becomes broken, stop may catch in retention aperture in receiver when slide reciprocates. If nose of stop or edge of retaining aperture becomes worn, stop is apt to slip and fail to hang bolt. In such a case stop or spring should be replaced and/or carbine sent to ordnance unit for repair.

CARBINE, CAL. .30, M1
SECTION V
IMMEDIATE ACTION AND STOPPAGES

39. OBJECT. — This section is designed to provide necessary instruction in the related subjects of immediate action and stoppages.

40. WHEN TAKEN UP. — Instruction in immediate action and stoppages will be completed before any firing is done by the individual.

41. IMMEDIATE ACTION. — *a. General.* — Immediate action is the unhesitating application of a probable remedy for a stoppage. Immediate action deals with the method of reducing stoppages and not the cause. It is taught as an unhesitating manual operation to be applied to reduce stoppages without detailed consideration of their causes.

b. Procedure. — (1) If the loaded carbine fails to fire when the trigger is pulled, count to "20" to allow for a hangfire, and then pull the operating slide handle to its rearmost position ejecting the round. Release the operating slide handle and if the bolt goes fully home, aim and fire.

CAUTION: When pulled to the rear, operating slide handle will be grasped by the little finger, with palm of hand facing up, to guard against injury should the cartridge fire late and actuate the operating mechanism while the operating slide is being retracted.

(2) If the bolt cannot be fully locked in (1) above, pull the operating slide handle to the rear. Check for a battered round, dirt, or obstruction on the face of the bolt, in the chamber, or in the locking lug recesses. Discard the battered round; remove the obstruction. Reload, aim, and fire.

(3) *The carbine fires but fails to feed.* — Keep the carbine in action by working the operating slide handle as it is still an effective combat weapon. A detailed examination for the malfunction may be made later when time permits.

(4) *Trigger fails to move forward when released due to broken or disengaged trigger spring.* — Push trigger forward manually after each shot, until time permits examination and correction. (Refer to paragraph 38 *b* (2).

42. STOPPAGES. — *a. General.* — While immediate action and stoppages are closely related as to subject matter, the former is treated separately to emphasize its importance as an automatic and definite procedure to be applied to overcome stoppages. Proper care of the carbine before, during, and after firing will usually eliminate stoppages. Stoppages which cannot be remedied by the application of immediate action can best be eliminated if the soldier has an understanding of the functioning of the weapon and the causes of stoppages.

b. Failure to fire. — (1) *Causes.* — Failures to fire are generally caused by:

(a) Defective ammunition.

(b) Defective firing pin.

(c) Bolt not fully closed when hammer strikes firing pin.

(2) *Action.* — *(a)* If the primer of a round is deeply indented, the round is defective. Discard the round. If the primer is not indented or but very lightly indented, the firing pin may be short or broken or the bolt may not have been fully closed. Check for dirt or some obstruction which does not permit the bolt to lock fully. Remove the obstruction. If the carbine is clean and lubricated, check the firing pin. Replace it if defective.

(b) Removal of a broken firing pin. — If the carbine fails to fire and the operating slide handle cannot be moved to the rear by a sharp blow with the heel of the hand, the firing pin may be broken, and having come out of its seat in the bolt it may have become wedged between the rear of the bolt and the top of the receiver. Remove the barrel and receiver assembly from the stock with trigger housing attached. Remove trigger housing, and firing pin should fall out. If barrel and receiver group or trigger housing cannot be removed easily, do not force. Turn upside down, shake, and work parts carefully until they will come apart.

c. *Failure to feed.* — (1) *Types.* — Failure to feed is caused by failure of the bolt to go far enough to the rear to pick up a new round. A failure to feed may have any one of a number of causes. It will generally result in one of the following types of stoppages:

(a) Those in which the bolt fails to go fully home.

(b) Those in which the bolt does go fully home.

(2) *Action to reduce stoppage of the first type.* — Stoppages of the first type may be caused by a battered round, dirt in the locking recesses, an obstruction on the face of the bolt, a dirty chamber, or a ruptured cartridge case, part of which remains in the chamber. Remove the battered round, dirt, or other obstruction; clean the chamber, or remove the ruptured cartridge case. Occasionally this stoppage may be caused by a magazine which has lost its spring tension, or in which the follower is defective, and does not hold the cartridge firmly in line. When this occurs, the cartridge will be found in the carbine with the nose of the bullet one side or the other of the entrance to the chamber. Remove the round; remove the magazine and discard it.

(3) *Action to reduce stoppage of the second type.* — Occasionally, when a stoppage of the second type occurs, the spent case is not ejected but is re-fed back into the chamber. This condition is caused by lack of lubrication, excessive friction of the moving parts, or lack of sufficient gas pressure due to the formation of carbon in the gas port. In any case the bolt has not moved far enough to the rear to permit proper functioning. The conditions are remedied by removing all carbon and thoroughly lubricating all parts as prescribed in Section IV — "Care, Cleaning and Lubrication."

d. Failure to extract. — (1) *Causes.* — Failures to extract are generally caused by:

(a) Extremely dirty chamber.

(b) Extremely dirty ammunition.

(c) Improper assembly of the rifle, such as failure to replace the extractor plunger and spring.

(d) Cartridge case chambered in a hot barrel.

(e) Broken extractor.

(2) *Action.* — (a) When a failure to extract occurs, the bolt may be found fully locked with a spent case in the chamber. Generally, most failures to extract can be remedied by pushing the operating slide fully forward and then pulling it smartly to the rear. If this does not remove the case, use a combination tool screw driver, or cleaning rod.

(b) Sometimes the empty case will be left in the chamber, the extractor ripping through the base of the cartridge. When this occurs the bolt generally will attempt to feed a fresh cartridge into the chamber. It will then be necessary to remove this round before the spent case can be removed.

(c) Where a dirty chamber or dirty ammunition is indicated, clean the chamber and discard or clean very dirty ammunition. Faulty assembly or a broken extractor will cause recurring failures to extract. Replace missing or broken parts.

e. Other stoppages. — In the event of stoppages that are not mentioned above and that cannot be reduced, the carbine should be turned in for examination and repair.

f. If the trigger, when retracted, does not release the hammer, release trigger and retract it again. If trigger does not release, the trigger spring is probably broken or out of place. Carbine may still be fired by pushing trigger forward and then retracting in usual manner as directed in paragraph 41 *b* (4).

g. If hammer does not release when trigger is retracted, sear or hammer spring may be broken. Remove trigger housing group, examine and replace damaged parts.

ORGANIZATION SPARE PARTS AND ACCESSORIES

SECTION VI

ORGANIZATION SPARE PARTS AND ACCESSORIES

43. ORGANIZATION SPARE PARTS. — *a.* The parts of any carbine will in time become unserviceable through breakage or wear resulting from continuous usage, and for this reason spare parts are supplied. These are extra parts provided with the carbine for replacement of the parts most likely to fail, for use in making minor repairs, and in general, care of the carbine. They should be kept clean and lightly oiled to prevent rust. Sets of spare parts should be kept complete at all times. Whenever a spare part is taken from the set to replace a defective part in the carbine, the defective part removed should be repaired, or a new one procured, and replaced in the spare parts set as soon as possible. Parts that are carried complete should, at all times, be correctly assembled and ready for immediate assembly to the carbine. The allowance of organization spare parts is prescribed for the carbine in SNL B-28.

b. With the exception of replacements with the spare parts mentioned in *a* above, repairs or alterations to the carbine by using organizations are prohibited.

44. ACCESSORIES. — *a. General.* — Accessories include the tools required for assembling, disassembling, and cleaning the carbine, also the gun sling, covers and similar articles. Accessories should not be used for purposes other than those for which they are intended, and when not in use should be stored in the places or receptacles provided for them. There are a number of accessories, the names or general characteristics of which indicate their uses or application. Therefore, detailed descriptions or methods of use of such items are not outlined herein. Accessories of a special nature or those which have special uses are described below.

b. Brush and thong. — The brush and thong are used for cleaning the bore of the carbine.

c. Case, cleaning rod, cal. .30, M1. — This case is a fabric container sewed to form five pockets to hold the four sections of the cal. .30 jointed cleaning rod M1 and the cal. .30 cleaning brush M2. A web-shaped billet and buckle are sewed on the front of the case to secure the flap, and a web hanger with brass hook is sewed on the back of the case to secure it to the ammunition belt. (Will be used for rod M8.)

d. Rod, cleaning, jointed, cal. .30, M8, w/brush, cleaning, cal. .30, M2. —

(1) *Rod, cleaning, jointed, cal. .30, M8.* — The cleaning rod consists of two sections threaded together. Attached to end of one section is a swivel

handle to facilitate use of rod. The handle allows the rod to rotate with the twist of the barrel, and acts as a stop to prevent the opposite end of the rod from striking the face of the bolt when in use. The end opposite the handle is slotted for assembly of the cleaning patch and has a threaded hole to permit assembly of the cleaning brush M2.

(2) *Brush, cleaning, cal. .30, M2.* — The cleaning brush M2 is a brass wire brush composed of a twisted wire core which retains the brass wire bristles constituting the brush. The core is fastened to a threaded shank by which the brush is attached to the slotted end of the rod.

e. *Sling, carbine (Figure 21).* — The carbine sling is an olive-drab, cotton web strap, adjustable to the soldier using it. In one end are two button holes about 3¾ inches apart, through which a bronze button passes to form a loop. To the other end is attached a lock buckle through which the sling passes. The lock of this buckle can be released to allow the sling strap to slide through the buckle and then locked upon the strap to hold the adjustment thus attained. The button end of the sling passes around the oiler through the opening in the left side of the stock after the oiler has been positioned in an aperture on the right side of the stock near the butt. The button holes are then mated and the button passed through them to hold the oiler in the loop so formed. The outer end of the sling strap passes through the sling swivel attached to the left side of the front band. The oiler acts as an anchor pin for the rear end of the sling as well as a means for lubricating the carbine.

f. *Oiler, carbine (Figure 21).* — The oiler consists of a tube to hold lubricating oil, a steel ring or cap seat, and a threaded cap in which is positioned a rod, or dropper. The oiler also acts as an anchor pin for the sling as described in e above.

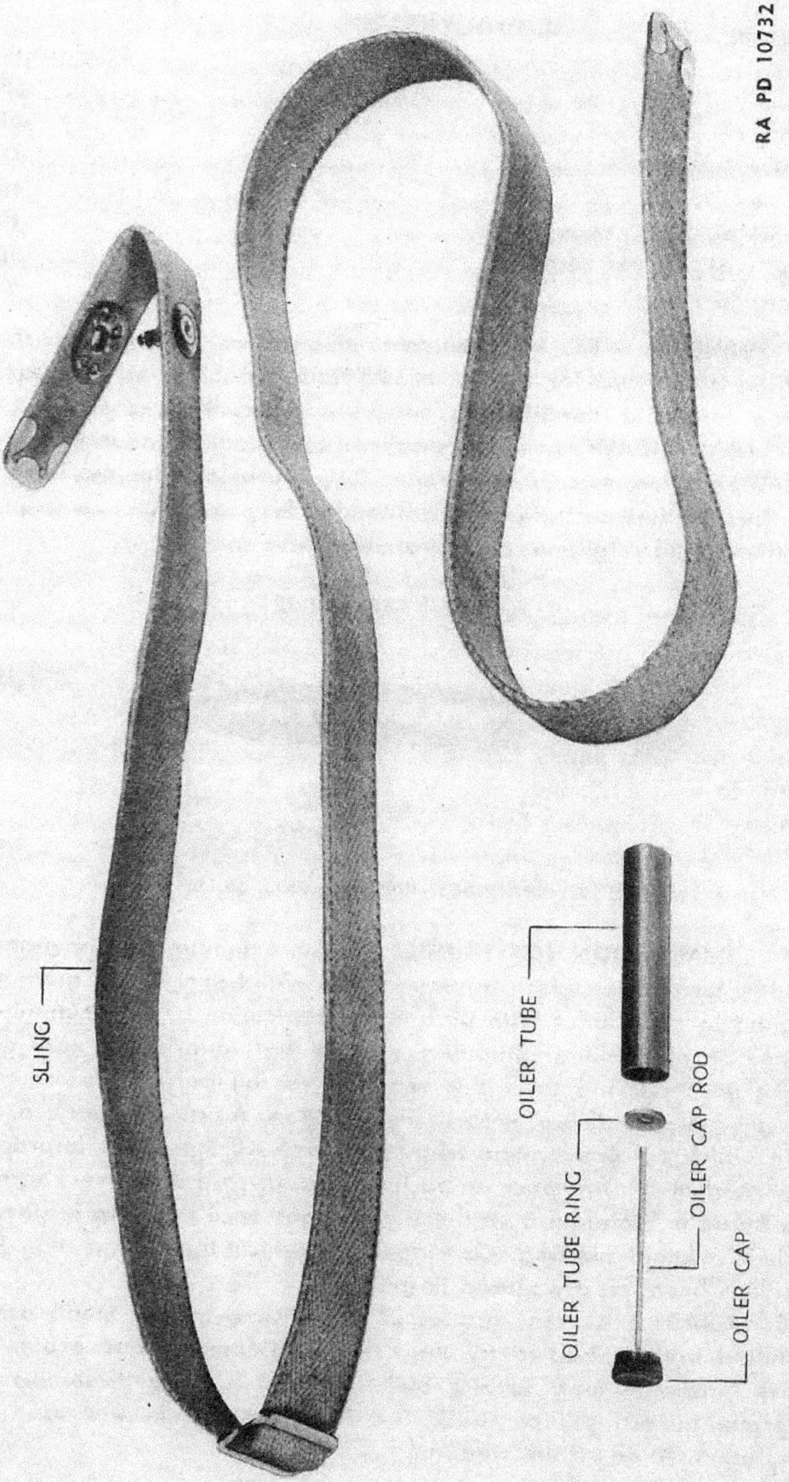

FIGURE 21 — SLING AND OILER — EXPLODED VIEW

CARBINE, CAL. .30, M1
SECTION VII
AMMUNITION

45. GENERAL. — The information in this section pertaining to the ammunition authorized for use in the CARBINE, cal. .30, M1, includes description, means of identification, care, use, and ballistic data.

46. CLASSIFICATION. — Only one type and model of cartridge, the CARTRIDGE, carbine, cal. .30, M1 (*Figure 22*), is provided for use in this carbine. This is a ball cartridge and is intended for use against personnel and light materiel targets at comparatively short ranges.

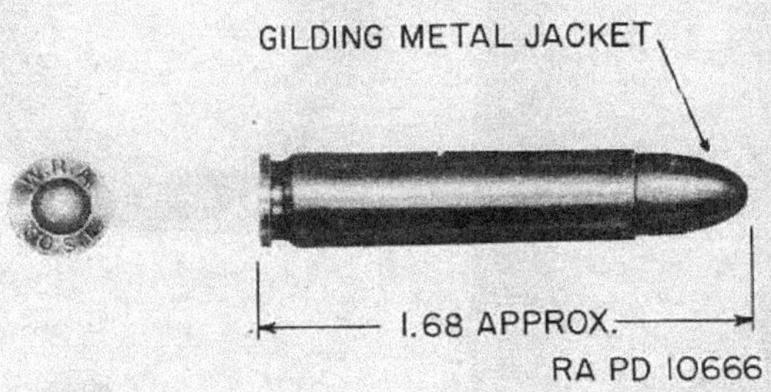

FIGURE 22 — CARTRIDGE, CARBINE, CAL. .30, M1

47. AMMUNITION LOT NUMBER. — When ammunition is manufactured, a lot number which becomes an essential part of the marking is assigned in accordance with pertinent specifications. This lot number is marked on all packing containers and on the identification card enclosed in each packing box. It is required for all purposes of record including grading and use, reports on condition, functioning, and accidents in which the ammunition might be involved. Since it is impracticable to mark this lot number on each individual cartridge, every effort will be made to maintain it with the cartridges once they are removed from their original packing. Cartridges for which the ammunition lot number has been lost are placed in grade 3.

48. GRADE. — Current grades of all existing lots of small arms ammunition are established by the Chief of Ordnance and are published in Ordnance Field Service Bulletin No. 3-5. Only those lots of appropriate grades will be fired. The following grades are used in grading ammunition for this weapon:

Grade R.

Grade 3. — Ammunition of this grade is unserviceable and will not be fired.

49. CARE, HANDLING, AND PRESERVATION. — a. Carbine ammunition, like all small arms ammunition, is not dangerous to handle. Care, however, must be exercised to keep the boxes from becoming broken or damaged. All broken boxes must be immediately repaired, and all markings transferred to the new parts of the box.

b. Ammunition boxes should not be opened until the cartridges are required for use. Ammunition if unpacked is apt to corrode, particularly in damp climates, thereby causing it to become unserviceable.

c. Ammunition should not be exposed to the direct rays of the sun nor to any source of excessive temperature as its firing qualities are liable to be affected seriously.

d. Ammunition should be carefully protected from mud, sand, dirt, and water. If it gets wet or dirty, it must be wiped off at once. Light corrosion, when present, should be removed. However, cartridges should not be polished to make them look better or brighter. Ammunition which is seriously corroded should not be used.

e. Carbine ammunition will not be fired until it has been positively identified by lot number and grade as published in the latest revision of, or change to Ordnance Field Service Bulletin No. 3-5.

50. CARTRIDGE, CARBINE, CAL. .30, M1. — a. This cartridge (*Figure 22*) can be identified by its characteristic shape and size, which differ considerably from all other cal. .30 cartridges. The nose of the bullet is round and the cartridge case is cylindrical throughout. The complete assembly is 1.68 inches in length and weighs approximately 195 grains.

b. The average velocity of the bullet at 53 feet from the muzzle is 1900 feet per second; the approximate maximum range 2000 yards; and the maximum chamber pressure 40,000 pounds per square inch.

c. The limit of accuracy at 100 yards is a mean radius of 1.5 inches and at 300 yards, 4 inches.

51. PRECAUTIONS IN FIRING. — Do not fire oiled or greased cartridges without first removing the oil or grease, nor those which have become heated due to exposure to the direct rays of the sun or other sources of high temperature. Such cartridges, if fired, may develop hazardous chamber pressures. See also paragraphs 31 f and 9 g, h and i.

CARBINE, CAL. .30, M1
SECTION VIII
MATERIEL AFFECTED BY GAS

52. PROTECTIVE MEASURES. — *a.* When materiel is in constant danger of gas attack, unpainted metal parts will be lightly coated with engine oil. Instruments are included among the items to be protected by oil from chemical clouds or chemical shells, but ammunition is excluded. Care will be taken that the oil does not touch the optical parts of instruments or leather or canvas fittings. Materiel not in use will be protected with covers as far as possible. Ammunition will be kept in sealed containers.

b. Ordinary fabrics offer practically no protection against mustard gas or lewisite. Rubber and oilcloth, for example, will be penetrated within a short time. The longer the period during which they are exposed, the greater the danger of wearing these articles. Rubber boots worn in an area contaminated with mustard gas may offer a grave danger to men who wear them several days after the bombardment. Impermeable clothing will resist penetration more than an hour, but should not be worn longer than this.

53. CLEANING. — *a.* All unpainted metal parts of materiel that have been exposed to any gas except mustard and lewisite must be cleaned as soon as possible with SOLVENT, dry cleaning, or ALCOHOL, denatured, and wiped dry. All parts should then be coated with engine oil.

b. Ammunition which has been exposed to gas must be thoroughly cleaned before it can be fired. To clean ammunition use AGENT, decontaminating, noncorrosive, or if this is not available, strong soap and cool water. After cleaning, wipe all ammunition dry with clean rags. *Do not use dry powdered AGENT, decontaminating (chloride of lime, used for decontaminating certain types of materiel) on or near ammunition supplies,* as flaming occurs through the use of chloride of lime on liquid mustard.

54. DECONTAMINATION. — For the removal of liquid chemicals (mustard, lewisite, etc.) from materiel, the following steps should be taken:

a. Protective measures. — (1) For all of these operations a complete suit of impermeable clothing and a service gas mask will be worn. Immediately after removal of the suit, a thorough bath with soap and water (preferably hot) must be taken. If any skin areas have come in contact with mustard, if even a very small drop of mustard gets into the eye, or if the vapor of mustard has been inhaled, it is imperative that complete

MATERIEL AFFECTED BY GAS

first-aid measures be given within 20 to 30 minutes after exposure. First-aid instructions are given in TM 9-850 and FM 21-40.

(2) Garments exposed to mustard will be decontaminated. If the impermeable clothing has been exposed to vapor only, it may be decontaminated by hanging in the open air, preferably in sunlight for several days. It may also be cleaned by steaming for 2 hours. If the impermeable clothing has been contaminated with liquid mustard, steaming for 6 to 8 hours will be required. Various kinds of steaming devices can be improvised from materials available in the field.

b. *Procedure.* — (1) Commence by freeing materiel of dirt through the use of sticks, rags, etc., which must be burned or buried immediately after this operation.

(2) If the surface of the materiel is coated with grease or heavy oil, this grease or oil should be removed before decontamination is begun. SOLVENT, dry cleaning, or other available solvents for oil should be used with rags attached to ends of sticks.

(3) Decontaminate the painted surfaces of the materiel with bleaching solution made by mixing one part AGENT, decontaminating (chloride of lime), with one part water. This solution should be swabbed over all surfaces. Wash off thoroughly with water, then dry and oil all surfaces.

(4) All unpainted metal parts and instruments exposed to mustard or lewisite must be decontaminated with AGENT, decontaminating, non-corrosive, mixed one part solid to fifteen parts solvent (ACETYLENE TETRACHLORIDE). If this is not available, use warm water and soap. Bleaching solution must not be used, because of its corrosive action. Instrument lenses may be cleaned only with PAPER, lens, tissue, using a small amount of ALCOHOL, ethyl. Coat all metal surfaces lightly with engine oil.

(5) In the event AGENT, decontaminating (chloride of lime) is not available, materiel may be temporarily cleaned with large volumes of hot water. However, mustard lying in joints or in leather or canvas webbing is not removed by this procedure and will remain a constant source of danger until the materiel can be properly decontaminated. All mustard washed from materiel in this manner lies unchanged on the ground, necessitating that the contaminated area be plainly marked with warning signs before abandonment.

(6) The cleaning or decontaminating of materiel contaminated with lewisite will wash arsenic compounds into the soil, poisoning any water supplies in the locality for either men or animals.

(7) Leather or canvas webbing that has been contaminated should be scrubbed thoroughly with bleaching solution. In the event this treatment is insufficient, it may be necessary to burn or bury such materiel.

(8) Detailed information on decontamination is contained in FM 21-40, TM 9-850, and TC 38, 1941, Decontamination.

55. SPECIAL POINTS PERTAINING TO CARBINE, CAL. .30, M1. —
The carbine should be completely disassembled for cleaning and decontamination, and special attention given to the points enumerated below:

    a. Bore and chamber.

    b. Piston and gas cylinder.

    c. Operating slide spring aperture in receiver.

    d. All spring, plunger, and other apertures.

    e. Sling and oiler aperture in stock.

    f. Receiver locking aperture in recoil plate.

    g. Barrel and receiver bed in stock and hand guard.

    h. Rear sight base and (beneath) spring.

    i. Sling.

By order of the Chief of Ordnance:

> J. K. CRAIN,
> Brig. Gen., Ord. Dept.,
> Chief of Field Service.

(O.O. 461/9826 Infantry)

REFERENCES

SECTION IX

REFERENCES

<table>
<tr><td></td><td>Paragraph</td></tr>
<tr><td>Standard nomenclature lists</td><td>56</td></tr>
<tr><td>Technical manuals</td><td>57</td></tr>
<tr><td>Field manuals</td><td>58</td></tr>
<tr><td>Technical circulars</td><td>59</td></tr>
<tr><td>Ordnance storage and shipment charts</td><td>60</td></tr>
</table>

56. STANDARD NOMENCLATURE LISTS. —

Ammunition, rifle and automatic gun	SNL T-1
Carbine, cal. .30, M1	SNL B-28
Cleaning, preserving and lubricating materials, recoil fluids, special oils, and similar items of issue	SNL K-1
Soldering, brazing and welding material, gases and related items	SNL K-2
Tools, maintenance, for repair of small and hand arms, and pyrotechnic projectors	SNL B-20
Truck, small arms repair, M1	SNL G-72
Current Standard Nomenclature Lists are as tabulated here. An up-to-date list of SNL's is maintained as the "Ordnance Publications for Supply Index"	OPSI

57. TECHNICAL MANUALS. —

Ammunition, general	TM 9-1900
Ammunition, small arms	TM 9-1990
Cleaning, preserving, lubricating and welding materials and similar items issued by the Ordnance Department	TM 9-850
Military chemistry and chemical agents	TM 3-215
Ordnance maintenance procedure — Materiel inspection and repair	TM 9-1100

58. FIELD MANUALS. —

Defence against chemical attack	FM 21-40

59. TECHNICAL CIRCULARS. —

Decontamination, 1941	TC No. 38

60. ORDNANCE STORAGE AND SHIPMENT CHARTS. —

Marking shipments of ordnance supplies	IOSSC - (b)
Ordnance storage and shipment chart — Group B — major items	OSSC B

INDEX

INDEX

INDEX

INDEX